Student´s Book 2

On Your Way

Building Basic Skills in English

Larry Anger

Marjorie Fuchs

Cheryl Pavlik

Margaret Keenan Segal

Longman

Executive Editor: Joanne Dresner
Development Editor: Nancy Perry
Production Editor: Catherine Hulbert
Book Design: Lynn Luchetti
Cover Illustration: Bill Schmidt
Production Director: Eduardo Castillo
Permissions and Photo Research: Esther Gottfried, Jari Flashner
Photo Credits: See page 124.

Reading and Writing Sections by Margaret Bonner

We wish to thank the following artists:
Storyline artist: Roman Szolkowski.
Interior artists: Beth J. Baum, Eulala Conner, Helen Davie, J & R Services,
Pam Johnson, Ron Sauter, Steven Shindler, Joel Snyder, Roman Szolkowski,
Nina Tallarico.

On Your Way Student's Book 2

Copyright © 1987 by Longman Inc.

ISBN: 0–582–90761–6

Longman Inc.
95 Church St.
White Plains, N.Y. 10601

Associated companies:
Longman Group Ltd., London; Longman Cheshire Pty., Melbourne; Longman Paul Pty.,
Auckland; Copp Clark Pitman, Toronto; Pitman Publishing Inc., New York

Library of Congress Cataloging–in–Publication Data
(Revised for vol. 2)
Anger, Larry, 1942-
   On your way.
   Book 2 by: Larry Anger, Marjorie Fuchs, Cheryl Pavlik,
Margaret Keenan Segal.
   Includes index.
   1. English language—Text-books for foreign speakers.
I. Pavlik, Cheryl, 1949-   . II. Segal, Margaret,
1950-   . III. Title.
PE1128.A53   1986   428.2′4   86-21524
ISBN 0-582-90760-8 (v. 1)

   89 90 9 8 7 6 5 4

Distributed in the United Kingdom by Longman Group Ltd., Longman House, Burnt Mill,
Harlow, Essex CM20 2JE, England, and by associated companies, branches, and
representatives throughout the world.

Printed in the U.S.A.

Consultants

JOSEPH BERKOWITZ
ESOL Program Coordinator
Miami Sunset Adult Education Center
Dade County
Miami, Florida

EILEEN K. BLAU
Associate Professor
Department of English
University of Puerto Rico
Mayaguez, Puerto Rico

CHERYL CREATORE
Curriculum Coordinator of ESL
Seneca Community College
Toronto, Ontario, Canada

JUDITH E. KLEEMAN
Manager Refugee Program
Houston Community College
Houston, Texas

JOANN LA PERLA
Director of Continuing Education and
    Community Services
Union County College
Cranford, New Jersey

VIRGINIA LOCASTRO
Lecturer
The University of Tsukuba
Japan

BARBARA MOTEN
Assistant Director – Project C3
Department of Adult Education
Detroit Public Schools
Detroit, Michigan

K. LYNN SAVAGE
Vocational ESL Resource Instructor
San Francisco Community College Centers
San Francisco, California

Contents

*Structure introduced in Student's Book 1 and reviewed here.

At the Street Market

1 Yolanda, Maria and Dave are at a street market. Listen to their conversation.

1

YOLANDA: Hi. My name's Yolanda Ruiz.

MARIA: Oh, hi. I'm Maria Gorska.

YOLANDA: Do you come here every day?

MARIA: No, only two or three times a week. I also work part time as a waitress. How about you?

YOLANDA: I'm here only on weekends. Gee, your T-shirts are great. Do you make them yourself?

MARIA: Yeah. I buy the shirts, and then I paint the designs.

2

DAVE: Hi, Yolanda.

YOLANDA: Oh, hi, Dave. Dave, I'd like you to meet Maria Gorska. Maria, this is Dave Carson.

3

DAVE: Hi, Ma—oh, I'm really sorry.

MARIA: That's OK. They're washable.

DAVE: Are you sure?

MARIA: Yeah, I always wash them. Don't worry about it.

2 Say *That's right* or *That's wrong*.

1. Yolanda and Maria go to the street market every day.
2. Maria sometimes works in a restaurant.
3. Yolanda likes Maria's T-shirts.
4. Maria can't wash her T-shirts.

3 Warm Up

Introduce yourself to the class.

Hi. My name's . . .

I'm from . . .

DEVELOP YOUR VOCABULARY

Mexico	Hong Kong
Poland	. . .

Practice

A.

I You We They	teach live don't live	
He She	teaches lives doesn't live	nearby.

Where	do	you they	work?
	does	he she	

Do	you they			I we they	do.		I we they	don't.
Does	he she	have any children?	Yes,	he she	does.	No,	he she	doesn't.

1 Who are these people and what do they do? Listen and match the people with their pictures.

1. *b* 2. ___ 3. ___ 4. ___ 5. ___ 6. ___ 7. ___ 8. ___

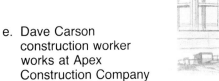

a. Maria Gorska
fashion designer, also
works part time
as a waitress

b. Barbara Gorska
computer programmer
works at High-Tech
Corporation

c. Steve Carson
teacher, teaches math
at Lincoln High School

d. Julie Carson
carpenter, makes tables
and chairs

e. Dave Carson
construction worker
works at Apex
Construction Company

f. Yolanda Ruiz
homemaker, also
makes jewelry

g. Roberto Ruiz
and Johnny Castillo
musicians, play in a band

h. Ricky Ruiz
and Lynn Carson
students, go to Wilson
Elementary School

2 Now talk about the people from Exercise 1 like this:

Maria Gorska is a fashion designer. She also works part time as a waitress.

3 Tell a classmate what you do.

A: What kind of work do you do?
B: I *work in a factory.* I *make calculators.*
   OR   I'm *a taxi driver.*

4 Listen to Yolanda and Maria's conversation. Complete it with the correct form of the verbs.

MARIA: Does Dave _Come_ here every day?
            $\overline{\quad 1 \quad}$

YOLANDA: Almost every day. He _____ nearby, so he often _____ here for lunch.
                              $\overline{\quad 2 \quad}$ $\overline{\quad 3 \quad}$

MARIA: _____ he live around here?
            $\overline{\quad 4 \quad}$

YOLANDA: No, he _____ on 85th Street. And I can guess your next question. No, he
                   $\overline{\quad 5 \quad}$

            _____ married, and he _____ _____ a girlfriend.
            $\overline{\quad 6 \quad}$ $\overline{\quad 7 \quad}$ $\overline{\quad 8 \quad}$

MARIA: I guess I *am* interested in him. _____ you know him well?
                                              $\overline{\quad 9 \quad}$

YOLANDA: Not really. He _____ in a band with my husband, and we joke around a lot.
                        $\overline{\quad 10 \quad}$

            He seems nice.

5 Complete these questions with *are* or *do.*

1. Where _are_ you from?
2. _____ you live around here?
3. _____ you married?
4. _____ you have any children?

5. What _____ you do for a living?
6. Where _____ you work?
7. _____ you like your job?

Now interview a classmate. Ask the questions above and write his or her answers.

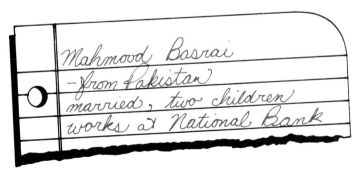

Mahmood Basrai
- from Pakistan
married, two children
works at National Bank

6 Now introduce the person you interviewed to the class. Tell a few things about the person like this:

I'd like you to meet Mahmood Basrai. He's from Pakistan. He's married, and he has two children. He works . . .

Just for Fun _____

7 Make a statement about someone in the class. Your classmates have to guess who you are talking about like this:

A: She works part time in a factory.
B: Is it Mei-ling?
A: No, it isn't.
C: Is it Jackie?
A: Yes, it is.

B.

I	work cook	at night. in the morning/afternoon/evening. on Saturday (mornings). on weekends. during the day/week.

1 Listen to Yolanda talk about her life. Then match her activities with the times she does them.

1. __d__ stays home with her kids
2. _____ sells jewelry at a street market
3. _____ cooks and cleans
4. _____ makes jewelry
5. _____ has a class in jewelry-making
6. _____ watches TV

a. on weekends
b. at night
c. every day
d. during the week
e. on Monday and Wednesday afternoons
f. in the morning

2 Now talk about Yolanda.

A: What does Yolanda do *on weekends?*
B: She *sells jewelry at a street market.*

5

C.

I	always usually generally	do the dishes.
I'm	often rarely never	at home.

1   Look at the chart. What do you do on weekends? What do you do during the week? Ask a classmate what he or she does and take notes.

A: What do you usually do in your free time during the week?

B: I *often go to the movies.*

A: How about on weekends?

B: Well, I *sometimes go dancing.*

A: Do you do anything else?

B: . . .

Reiko
week - often goes to the movies
weekend - often goes dancing

How Do You Spend Your Free Time?

	weekends	weekdays		weekends	weekdays
Sports			**Home relaxation**		
go swimming	☐	☐	watch TV	☐	☐
go bowling	☐	☐	read books	☐	☐
play soccer	☐	☐	read magazines	☐	☐
play baseball	☐	☐	or newspapers	☐	☐
. . .			play games	☐	☐
			listen to music	☐	☐
Outside entertainment			have friends over	☐	☐
go to the movies	☐	☐	spend time with the family		
go dancing	☐	☐	. . .		
go shopping	☐	☐			
go out to eat	☐	☐			
visit friends	☐	☐			
. . .					

2   Now write about a classmate's free-time activities. Then tell the class like this:

Reiko often goes to the movies during the week. She sometimes goes dancing on weekends. She also . . .

3 Review and Build

Choose the correct word to complete these questions.

1. Do you have friends over __*on*__ weekends?
   _{in/on}

2. Do you play any sports _____ Saturdays?
   _{in/on}

3. What do you usually do _____ Sunday mornings?
   _{at/on}

4. Do you go to school _____ the afternoon?
   _{in/on}

5. Do you ever watch TV _____ the day?
   _{on/during}

6. Do you ever go out to eat _____ the evening?
   _{in/at}

7. What do you do _____ night _____ the week?
   _{at/on} _{on/during}

Now ask a classmate the questions.

1. A: Do you have friends over on weekends?
   B: Yes, *we often* do.
      OR   No, *I work on weekends, so I see my friends during the week.*

4 Choose six activities from the chart on page 6 and find out how often a classmate does them.

A: How often do you *go dancing?*
B: Oh, *about once a week.*
A: How often do you *watch TV?*
B: *Almost every night.*

DEVELOP YOUR VOCABULARY

almost every day / week
about twice a month
about three times a year
once in a while
· · ·

PUT IT ALL TOGETHER
Dave and Yolanda are talking at the market. Listen and complete their conversation.

DAVE: What do you know about Maria?

YOLANDA: Well, she *paints* beautiful T-shirts.
                      ₁

DAVE: Yes, I know that. What else _____ she _____ ?
                                    ₂   ₃

YOLANDA: She also _____ part time as a waitress.
                   ₄

DAVE: _____ _____ does she _____ to the street market?
          ₅   ₆   ₇

YOLANDA: Two or three times _____ _____ . Why?
                              ₈   ₉

DAVE: Oh, she seems nice, that's all.

ON YOUR OWN
Discuss these questions with your classmates.

1 Are there street markets in your country? If so, what kinds of things do they sell?

2 Do you ever go to street markets? Do you like them? What are the advantages and disadvantages of shopping at street markets?

Reading

Our Town Magazine: INTERVIEW

Joseph Mecca is a taxi driver.
In this interview, he talks about his work.

Joe Mecca, ready for work

OUR TOWN: Joe, I see you're very happy in your job. What do you like about your work?

JOE: I meet a lot of colorful people, so my work is always interesting.

(5) OUR TOWN: When do you usually work?

JOE: From 5:00 in the afternoon until midnight. I make good money that way.

OUR TOWN: Why?

JOE: At 5:00, I pick up the business people. Around 11:00,
(10) people go home from dinner and the movies. So, I have two busy times.

OUR TOWN: What do you do during the day?

JOE: I go to school. I study part time. I like this job, but I want to be a computer programmer.

(15) OUR TOWN: What do you dislike about your work?

JOE: I sit all the time, so I'm getting fat. And I never see my girlfriend. She works from 9:00 to 5:00.

1 Comprehension. Answer the questions about Joe's job.

1. Why does Joe like his job?
2. When does he usually work?
3. What does he do in the daytime?
4. What does he dislike about his job?

2 Vocabulary building. Choose the word or phrase that means the *opposite* of the one underlined.

1. *(line 3)* I meet a lot of colorful people.
   a. interesting
   b. boring
   c. nice

2. *(line 6)* I make good money.
   a. a lot of
   b. very little
   c. bad

3. *(line 13)* I study part time.
   a. full time
   b. never
   c. sometimes

4. *(line 15)* What do you dislike about your job?
   a. do
   b. hate
   c. like

3 Sentence logic. Connect the two parts of these sentences.

A

1. _d_ Joe meets a lot of colorful people,
2. ____ At 5:00,
3. ____ At 11:00,
4. ____ Joe likes his job,
5. ____ Joe never sees his girlfriend,

B

a. but he wants to be a computer programmer.
b. people go home from dinner and the movies.
c. because she works from 9:00 to 5:00 and he works at night.
d. so his job is interesting.
e. he picks up the business people.

—*Writing*—

Skill: Connecting ideas with *and, but* and *so*
Task: Writing a note

We often leave someone a message by writing a short note. You can connect the ideas in your note with *and, but* and *so.*

> **Note:** *So* means the second idea is the result of the first idea.
> *It rained, so I took your umbrella with me.*
> (Because it rained, I took your umbrella.)

Practice writing short notes. Choose one sentence from column A and one sentence from column B. Connect them using *and, but* or *so.*

A	B
1. Dave is sick today,	a. she delivered it to your home this morning.
2. Mark Wolski of National Bank called,	b. please call Acme Cab for her.
3. Ms. Carson finished your new table yesterday,	c. she can meet with you on Monday.
4. Barbara Gorska can't meet with you tomorrow,	d. he can't come to lunch.
5. Ms. Jones wants a taxi at 5 P.M.,	e. he said he needs your account number.

From the desk of
Sylvia Salazar

Dave is sick today, so he can't come to lunch.

For pronunciation exercises for Unit 1, see page 110.

1 **Yolanda is at the street market. She is talking to a customer. Listen to their conversation.**

1

YOLANDA: May I help you?

CUSTOMER 1: Yes. Where can I get something to drink around here?

YOLANDA: There's a soda machine inside.

CUSTOMER 1: Oh, do you have change for a dollar?

YOLANDA: Sure. Here you are.

CUSTOMER 1: Thanks.

2

CUSTOMER 1: Those necklaces are nice. How much are they?

YOLANDA: The silver ones are $35, and the other ones are $20.

CUSTOMER 1: Can I see the silver one?

YOLANDA: Which one?

CUSTOMER 1: The one with the blue stone. . . . Can I try it on?

YOLANDA: Yes. There's a mirror right there.

CUSTOMER 2: Excuse me, miss, can I see that necklace?

3

YOLANDA: Sure. Would you like to try. . . . Miss. . . miss? Hey, miss. Hey! Stop that woman! She took my necklace!

CUSTOMER 2: What happened?

YOLANDA: She stole a necklace!

2 **Say *That's right* or *That's wrong*.**

1. Yolanda didn't have change for a dollar.
2. A customer asked about a silver necklace.
3. The customer didn't pay for the necklace.

3 **Warm Up**

Ask where you can buy something to eat or drink near your school.

A: Excuse me. Where can I get something to eat (drink) around here?

B: There's a *snack bar downstairs*.

DEVELOP YOUR VOCABULARY

grocery store	upstairs
cafeteria	on the fourth floor
soda machine	across the street
. . .	. . .

Practice

A.

You She They	stole wanted		a necklace.
	didn't	steal want	

What happened?	Someone stole a necklace.
Who stole the necklace?	Janet did.

Spelling note:

regular past tense verbs

want + *ed* → wanted

lov~~e~~ + *ed* → loved

rob + *b* + *ed* → robbed

cr~~y~~ + *ed* → cried

For a list of irregular verbs, see page 114.

1 Write the past tense forms.

1. take   t o o k
2. is   w _ _
3. come   c _ m _
4. bring   b _ o _ _ h _
5. try   tr _ _ _

6. blow   bl _ _
7. like   l _ k _ d
8. stop   _ t _ p _ _ d
9. drive   dr _ v _
10. run   r _ _

2 Look at the pictures and tell what happened.

1. A: What happened?
   B: Someone *stole a necklace.*

1. steal a necklace

2. run after the thief

3. shout for help

4. try to stop the thief

5. blow a whistle

6. call the police

7. come to ask questions

8. drive Yolanda to the police station

3 Now find out who did the things in Exercise 2.

1. A: Who *stole the necklace?*
    B: *Janet Garvey* did.

Key to the people in Exercise 2

1. Janet Garvey   2. Evelyn Johnson   3. Ha Pham   4. Paul Levin
5. Kim Yee   6. Henry Brazinski   7. Officer Ortiz   8. Officer O'Brien

---

4 Make negative statements about these people.

1. Evelyn Johnson ___*didn't steal*___ the necklace. Janet Garvey did.

2. Paul Levin _____ the police. Henry Brazinski did.

3. Ha Pham _____ the whistle. Kim Yee did.

4. Kim Yee _____ for help. Ha Pham did.

5. Officer Ortiz _____ Yolanda to the police station. Officer O'Brien did.

6. Henry Brazinski _____ after the thief. Evelyn Johnson did.

B.

How old			28 (years old).
How tall	was she?	She was	5 foot 5. 5 feet 5 inches tall.
What color	were her eyes?	They were blue.	
	was her hair?	It was blond.	

For Your Information

Measurement

The English System for height uses feet and inches. There are twelve inches in a foot.

English to metric			*Metric to English*		
1 inch (in. or ")	=	2.54 centimeters	1 meter	=	39.37 inches
1 foot (ft. or ')	=	0.254 meter		=	3.28 feet

The English system for weight uses pounds.

English to metric			*Metric to English*		
1 pound (lb.)	=	.45 kilogram	1 kilogram	=	2.2 pounds

For more weights and measures, see page 115.

1 Yolanda is giving the police a description of the thief. Listen and choose the correct features.

Sex:	M	(F)
Age:	24	28
Height:	5'4"	6'4"
Weight:	130 lbs.	113 lbs.
Eyes:	blue	hazel
Hair:	blond	brown
Other features:	glasses	pierced ears

2 Now pretend you are giving the police descriptions of these people.

1. POLICE OFFICER: How old was *he?*
   YOU: *Forty-two.*
   POLICE OFFICER: How tall was *he?*
   YOU: *Six foot three.* And *he* weighed about *190 pounds.*
   POLICE OFFICER: What color were *his* eyes?
   YOU: *Brown.*
   POLICE OFFICER: What color was *his* hair?
   YOU: *Black.* Oh, and *he had a mustache.*

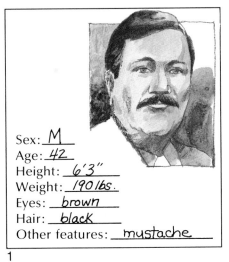

Sex: _M_
Age: _42_
Height: _6'3"_
Weight: _190 lbs._
Eyes: _brown_
Hair: _black_
Other features: _mustache_

1

Sex: _m_
Age: _38_
Height: _5'8"_
Weight: _240 lbs._
Eyes: _blue_
Hair: _blond_
Other features: _beard_

2

Sex: _F_
Age: _29_
Height: _5'6"_
Weight: _130 lbs._
Eyes: _hazel_
Hair: _dark brown_
Other features: _glasses_

3

3 Review and Build

You're going to meet someone who doesn't know you. Pretend you're talking on the phone and describe yourself.

A: What do you look like?
B: Well, I'm *5'9".* I have *hazel* eyes and *dark brown* hair. I also have a *mustache* and *wear glasses.*

C.

The ring	**with the blue stone** **from Mexico** **in the case** **on the table**	is beautiful.
The man	**with the glasses** **on the right**	is Paul Levin.

1 Look at the pictures. Give your opinion about these things from the street market.

A: I think *that ring from China is pretty.*
B: I agree.   OR   Oh, I don't. I think *it's ordinary.*

You can use these adjectives:

awful   beautiful   cheap   expensive   ordinary   terrific   ugly   wonderful

rings

1a. from China   **1b.** from Mexico

sweaters

2a. from Ireland   **2b.** from Italy

T-shirts

3a. with short sleeves   **3b.** with long sleeves

earrings

4a. on the case

4b. in the case

Just for Fun

2 A group of people at the market are talking to Yolanda about the robbery.
Can you identify them?

A: The man *in the white T-shirt* is *Paul Levin.*
B: That's right. And the woman . . .
    OR   No, it isn't. The man *with the glasses*
    is *Paul.*

If you need help identifying the people, look back at pages 3, 11 and 12.

D.

How much are the necklaces?	**The** silver **one** is $35. **The** gold **ones** are $85. **The other ones** are $20.
Which one do you want to buy?	**The one** with the blue stone.

1 Ask the prices of the things in Exercise 1 on page 14.

1a. A: How much *is this ring?*
    B: Which *one?*
    A: The *one from China.*
    B: *It's $45.*

Just for Fun _____

2   What are the thieves saying?

1. A: Take *the wallets.*
   B: Which *ones?*
   A: The *brown leather ones.*

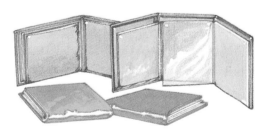

1. brown leather wallets / red leather wallets

4. silver watch / gold watch

2. diamond bracelet / gold bracelet

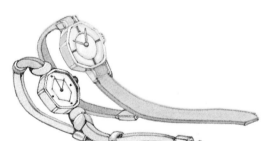

5. wool scarves / silk scarves

3. vase in the case / vase on the case

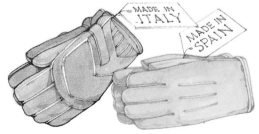

6. gloves from Italy / gloves from Spain

Life Skills

Shopping and money

1   Look at the directory. Find out where to get things in Bergendale's Department Store.

BERGENDALE'S DEPARTMENT STORE
DIRECTORY

Children's Department—4
   boys' and girls' clothes
Electronics Department—4
   TV's, stereos, radios, calculators,
   VCR's, computers, electronic games
Furniture Department—6
   couches, chairs, tables, beds
Housewares Department—5
   dishes, small electric appliances,
   silverware
Jewelry Department—1
   necklaces, earrings, rings, watches

Juniors' Department—3
   young women's dresses,
   sportswear
Linen Department—5
   towels, sheets, blankets
Men's Department—1
   suits, sportswear, coats, ties
Misses' Department—2
   women's dresses, sportswear
Shoe Department—3
   shoes, boots, socks

YOU: Excuse me. Where can I get *a blender?*
CLERK: In the *housewares* department.
YOU: Where's that?
CLERK: On the *fifth floor.*

2   What is the sale price of these items?

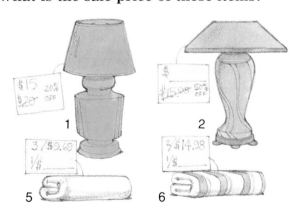
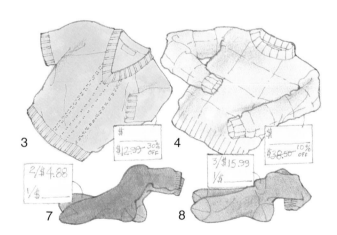

Now ask the prices of the items above.

1. YOU: How much is this *lamp?*
    CLERK: Which one?
    YOU: The *red* one.
    CLERK: It's on sale for *$15.*

6. YOU: How much are these *sheets?*
    CLERK: Which ones?
    YOU: The ones *with the blue stripes.*
    CLERK: They're *two for $14.98,* so they're
            $7.49 each.

3 Pretend you're shopping with a friend. Ask to see something and try it on.

1. CLERK: May I help you?
    YOU: Yes, can I see that *pair of gloves*, please?
    CLERK: Here you are.
    YOU: Can I try *them* on?
    CLERK: Sure.
    YOU: How *do they* look?
    FRIEND: *They look great.*

DEVELOP YOUR VOCABULARY

They look
It looks
{ kind of weird.
pretty nice.
OK.
. . .

I don't like it (them) very much.

1. pair of gloves   2. belt   3. pair of sunglasses   4. jacket   5. pair of sneakers   6. hat

4 Buy the item you tried on. Pay by check.

YOU: I'll take this *pair of gloves*.
CLERK: Is that cash or charge?
YOU: Do you take checks?
CLERK: Yes, with two pieces of ID.
YOU: Here's my *driver's license* and
         student ID.
CLERK: That's fine. Just make the check out to
         Bergendale's Department Store.

cash   check   identification (ID)
              credit card

5 Dictation

Yolanda's friend Judy Chen is shopping at Bergendale's Department Store. Listen to the conversation. Then listen again and write it.

JUDY: _____ ?
                              1
CLERK: _____ ?
                              2
JUDY: _____ .
                              3
CLERK: _____ .
                              4
JUDY: _____ ?
                              5
CLERK: _____ .
                              6

Now pretend you want to buy the item. Continue the conversation.

ON YOUR OWN
Think about Yolanda's experience with the thief. Then discuss these questions with your classmates.

1 Did anyone ever steal anything from you? What did you do? How did you feel?

2 What are some things you can do so that you don't get robbed?

For pronunciation exercises for Unit 2, see page 110.

REVIEW 1

1 Read this paragraph about Yolanda Ruiz and complete it with an appropriate verb.

Yolanda Ruiz _works_ very hard. She _____ n't have a lot of free time.
During the week she _____ home with her children. She _____ jewelry in the
morning and _____ a class in jewelry-making on Monday and Wednesday
afternoons. On weekends she _____ the jewelry at a street market. In the evenings
she and her husband _____ TV or _____ to music. They _____ n't go out very
much. They usually _____ to bed early because they are both very tired.

2 Write questions about Dave.

1. A: _What does Dave do_ ?
   B: He's a construction worker.
2. A: _____?
   B: At Apex Construction Co.
3. A: _____?
   B: No, he doesn't. He plays the drums.
4. A: _____?
   B: Yes, he does. He goes to the street market almost every day for lunch.
5. A: _____?
   B: Three times a week. He practices with Yolanda's husband.

3 Match the questions in column A with the answers in column B. Complete the answers.

A	B
1. _c_ Do Maria and Yolanda go to the market every day?	a. Yes, he _____.
2. ___ Does Dave play in a band?	b. No, she _____.
3. ___ Does Yolanda make jewelry?	c. No, they _don't_.
4. ___ Does Maria play in a band?	d. Yes, we _____.
5. ___ Do you and your classmates speak English in class?	e. Yes, she _____.

4 Put these words in the correct order.

1. read   the   I   always   newspaper

I always read the newspaper.

2. on   I   weekends   study
3. never   She   late   comes
4. You   right   usually   are
5. in   She   afternoon   works   the
6. to   We   often   go   the   movies
7. at   They   always   are   home
8. every   day   come   here   We

18

5 Complete these sentences. Use one of the time expressions in the box.

every~~day~~	always	on weekends
never	in the morning	in the evening

1. She doesn't work _every day_. She's only at the street market on weekends.
2. Dave _____ smokes. He hates cigarettes.
3. You can only call her _____, between 7:00 and 8:00 P.M.
4. I never work _____. Saturday and Sunday are my days off.
5. We _____ take the bus, because we don't like the subway.
6. I have a cup of tea _____, an hour before lunch.

6 Complete these sentences. Use the past tense of the verbs.

1. Yesterday Yolanda _was_ at the market.
   (be)
2. A customer _____ to try on a necklace.
   (want)
3. Another customer _____ about some earrings.
   (ask)
4. Then the first customer _____ the necklace.
   (steal)
5. The police _____ to the market.
   (go)
6. They _____ for the thief, but they _____ her.
   (look)   (find -neg.)
7. Finally, one of the police officers _____ Yolanda to the station.
   (drive)

7 Match the questions in column A with the answers in column B.

A	B
1. _d_ How old is she?	a. They're green.
2. _f_ How tall is she?	b. It's dark brown.
3. _a_ What color are her eyes?	c. She makes jewelry.
4. _b_ What color is her hair?	d. 31.
5. _c_ What does she do?	e. Two times a week.
6. _e_ How often does she come here?	f. 5 feet 6 inches.

8 Complete this conversation. Use _one_ or _ones_.

SALESPERSON: Can I help you?

CUSTOMER: Yes. I'd like to see that blouse.

SALESPERSON: Which _one_ ?
                    1

CUSTOMER: The _____ with the red and purple flowers.
               2

SALESPERSON: This _____ ?
                  3

CUSTOMER: Yes. That's the _____. Are those sweaters on sale too?
                         4

SALESPERSON: The _____ on the case are on sale, but the _____ in the case aren't.
               5   6

CUSTOMER: I see. Can I try _____ on?
                           7

SALESPERSON: Of course.

3 Would You Like a Ride Home?

1 Dave met Maria at the street market. Listen to their conversation.

1

DAVE: Would you like a ride home?
MARIA: Yes, thanks. I'd appreciate it.
DAVE: Did Yolanda get her necklace back?
MARIA: No, she didn't. The police are still looking for the thief.

2

MARIA: Uh, Dave, you're going kind of fast. Can you slow down a little, please?
DAVE: Sure. Sorry.
MARIA: Yolanda told me you play in a rock band.
DAVE: Yeah, I play the drums.
MARIA: Really! I love rock. In fact, I went to the Tina Turner concert last weekend.
DAVE: Lucky you. I couldn't go. Did you—
MARIA: Dave, what are you doing?
DAVE: I'm just turning.
MARIA: But that car! Be careful!
DAVE: Don't worry. I see it.

3

DAVE: So, did you enjoy the concert?
MARIA: Yeah. Tina Turner's a great performer.
DAVE: Yes, she is. Say, would you like to go to a movie tomorrow night?
MARIA: I'd love to. But... can we take the bus?
DAVE: Come on, my driving isn't *that* bad!

2 Answer the questions.

1. Who took Maria home?
2. What kind of music does Dave play?
3. Does Dave like Tina Turner?
4. Why does Maria want to take the bus to the movies?

3 Warm Up

Ask a classmate to do something for you.

A: Can you *help me with my homework?*
B: Sure.   OR   Sorry, but *I don't have the time.*

DEVELOP YOUR VOCABULARY

lend me *a pen ($5.00)*
explain this to me
change seats with me
get me *a can of soda*
. . .

─Practice─

A.

Did	you he she they	**call** the police?	Yes,	I we he	**did.**
			No,	she they	**didn't.**
When did			Yesterday morning.		

1 What happened after the robbery? Look at the picture and ask and answer questions. Answer with *I think* if you aren't sure.

1. Yolanda / go to the police station
A: Did Yolanda go to the police station?
B: Yes, she did.

2. Maria / go to the police station with Yolanda
A: Did Maria go to the police station with Yolanda?
B: No, she didn't.   OR   No, I don't think she did.

3. police / arrest Yolanda
4. Yolanda / describe the thief
5. police / write a report
6. Yolanda / look through a book of photographs
7. Yolanda / identify the thief

2 Review and Build

Pretend it's Sunday, April 10, 1988. Janet Garvey is a suspect for robbery. Look at the police report and ask and answer questions like this:

A: When did Janet Garvey *go to jail?*
B: *Two years ago.*

Student B can use these words:

yesterday   yesterday morning   last year   *two* months (years) ago

Name: *Janet Garvey*	Address: *242 Fulton Street*	
February 10, 1986	*went to jail for robbery*	
February 15, 1987	*escaped from jail*	
September 1987	*got a job as a filing clerk*	
February 1988	*lost her job*	
April 9, 1988	*went to the street market*	
April 9, 1988	*sold necklace to shopkeeper*	

3 It's now two days after the robbery. Look at the pictures and talk about what Yolanda and Janet did yesterday.

A: What did *Yolanda* do yesterday?
B: She *went to the street market.*
A: What else did she do?
B: She . . .

YOLANDA

1

2

3

JANET

1

2

3

4 Find out if a classmate did anything special recently.

A: Did you do anything special *last night?*
B: Yes, I did. I *went to a party.* How about you?
   OR   No, I didn't. I just *stayed home and cleaned the house.* How about you?
A: I . . .

DEVELOP YOUR VOCABULARY

went to a wedding	did errands
ran in a marathon	visited relatives
went on a picnic	. . .

B.

Could you sleep last night?	Yes, I could. No, I couldn't.
Yolanda couldn't catch the thief, but she could describe her.	

1 Ask and answer questions about these people:

1. A: Could Yolanda sleep last night?
   B: No, she couldn't.

1. Yolanda / sleep   2. Yolanda / identify the thief   3. police / find Janet Garvey   4. Janet / sell the necklace

2 Talk about what you could or couldn't do five years ago.

A: Could you *speak English* five years ago?
B: Yes, I could, but I couldn't *write a letter in English.*   OR   No, I couldn't, but I could *understand a little.*

DEVELOP YOUR VOCABULARY

play the piano	ride a bicycle
use a computer	. . .
drive a car	

C.

What	**are** you	**doing?**	I'm **looking** out the window.
	is she		She's **watering** the flowers.

1 Maria's sister Barbara is blind—she can't see. She's asking her brother Peter what is happening on their street. What are they saying? Use the words in the box.

<del>play ball</del>	knock down a building
dance	water the flowers
jump rope	wash his car

BARBARA: Who's out on the street?
PETER: *Some boys.*
BARBARA: What *are they* doing?
PETER: *They're playing ball.*

construction workers   Mrs. Kaminsky

Mr. Ryan

teenagers   girls   boys

2 It's later in the day. Maria is talking to Yolanda on the phone. Read their conversation and write the questions.

MARIA: Hi, Yolanda, it's Maria. ____*How are you feeling*____ ?
                                                      1

YOLANDA: Well, I'm still a little upset about the robbery.

MARIA: _____ ?
                                            2

YOLANDA: Not much. I'm just having some tea. _____ ?
                                                                          3

MARIA: I'm cooking dinner.

YOLANDA: _____ ?
                                            4

MARIA: Spaghetti.

YOLANDA: What's that noise?

MARIA: Oh, there are some construction workers outside.

YOLANDA: It sounds terrible. _____ ?
                                                        5

MARIA: They're knocking down a building.

YOLANDA: I can't hear you. Call me back later.

MARIA: OK. Goodbye.

3 Find out what a classmate's friend or relative is doing now.

A: What's *your husband* doing now?

B: Let's see. It's *12:00. He*'s probably *eating his lunch.*

D.

Are you		Yes, I **am.**
Is he	**still working** at the grocery store?	No, he **isn't working** there **anymore.**

1 Listen to the conversations. What is each person doing now? What did they do in the past? Use *now* or *in the past* to describe each picture.

1. a. *now*   b. _____   2. a. _____   b. _____

3. a. _____   b. _____

2 Now ask a classmate about the past situations in Exercise 1.

1. A: How's *Dave? Is he* still *playing the piano?*
   B: No, *he isn't playing the piano* anymore.
   A: What's *he* doing now?
   B: *He's playing the drums.*

3 Find out what someone is doing these days.

A: What are you doing these days? Are you still
   working at the grocery store?
B: Yes, I am.   OR   No, I'm not *working there* anymore.

You can use these ideas:

living in . . .	working on weekends (at night)
living alone	studying . . .
living with . . .	having problems with . . .

PUT IT ALL TOGETHER
**Maria is calling Yolanda to find out how she is and to ask about the robbery.
Listen to their conversation and complete it.**

YOLANDA: Hello?

MARIA: Hi, Yolanda. This is Maria. *How* are you _____ ? _____ you sleep better
        <u>1</u>   <u>2</u>   <u>3</u>

        last night?

YOLANDA: Oh, I'm OK now. I'm not _____ upset _____ .
                                <u>4</u>   <u>5</u>

MARIA: That's good. _____ they _____ the thief?
                      <u>6</u>   <u>7</u>

YOLANDA: No, they're _____ _____ for her. But they _____ my necklace.
                     <u>8</u> <u>9</u>   <u>10</u>

MARIA: _____ did they _____ it?
        <u>11</u>   <u>12</u>

YOLANDA: Well, Janet Garvey _____ it to a shopkeeper. The shopkeeper _____
                            <u>13</u>   <u>14</u>

        Garvey's picture in the newspaper and _____ the police. Now, I just hope
                                              <u>15</u>

        they find Garvey!

ON YOUR OWN
**Dave and Maria both like rock music. What about you? Discuss these questions
with your classmates.**

1 What kinds of music do you like? Who is
   your favorite musician? Do you like to listen
   to records or to the radio? Do you ever go to
   concerts?

2 Do you play a musical instrument? If so,
   what do you play? Where did you learn to
   play?

Reading

Everybody's Talking About . . .
TINA TURNER

What's age got to do with it?

Tina Turner was born Anna Mae Bullock in 1940 in a small country town in Tennessee. She didn't like farm work, but she loved to sing (5) and dance. She got her first chance to perform with Ike Turner at the age of 16. She was a hit, and soon she and Ike were married.

During the 60's and early 70's, (10) the Ike and Tina Turner Revue performed in the United States, Europe, Japan and Africa. They recorded twenty albums and lived the lives of superstars, with a big (15) house and expensive cars.

But Ike and Tina had problems. Tina was the star onstage, but offstage Ike controlled everything, even her money. After a fight one (20) night in 1976, Tina left Ike. She had no money, but she said, "I felt proud. I felt strong. I felt like Martin Luther King."

After a year, Tina started singing (25) again. It took her a long time to rebuild her career. Things changed in 1981. She toured with the Rolling Stones, and people loved her. She recorded "Let's Stay (30) Together" in 1983, and the song sold more than a million records. She then recorded the best song of 1984, "What's Love Got to Do With It?"

(35) Tina's concerts are selling out everywhere. And now, almost 50, she isn't showing her age—she is showing that great talent and hard work never grow old.

1 Comprehension. Say *That's right* or *That's wrong.*

1. Tina Turner was born in New York.
2. Tina's first performance was a hit.
3. The Ike and Tina Turner Revue only toured Tennessee.
4. Tina and Ike had a lot of money, but they had problems.
5. Ike left Tina in 1976.
6. Tina rebuilt her career fast.
7. Tina's song "What's Love Got to Do With It?" won an award.

2 Vocabulary building. Choose the word that means the *same* as the one underlined.

1. (*line 7*) When a singer is a hit,
   a. people like her.
   b. people don't like her.
2. (*line 22*) When Tina felt proud, she felt
   a. good about her life.
   b. sad about her life.
3. (*line 26*) When Tina had to rebuild her career, she
   a. built it for the first time.
   b. built it again.
4. (*line 35*) When a concert sells out,
   a. there are no more tickets.
   b. people can still buy tickets.

3 Discussion. What do you think? Discuss your answers to the following questions with your classmates.

1. Why did Tina Turner say, "I felt proud. I felt strong. I felt like Martin Luther King"?

2. Tina Turner grew up on a farm, and then she became a superstar. Is a big change like that difficult?

3. Tina Turner became a big star when she was 46. Is that too old for a rock star?

Writing

**Skill: Organizing paragraphs using sentence connectors *first*, *then* and *now*
Task: Writing a postcard**

When you write a postcard, you want to tell a friend what you are doing on your trip. The connecting words *first*, *then* and *now* show the order that things happen.

EXAMPLE: *First* we went to a museum. *Then* we went sightseeing. *Now* we are relaxing in a café and writing postcards.

1   Finish writing this postcard. Put the verbs into the correct tense.

You can use these ideas:

go shopping	go to a movie / concert / bullfight
go sightseeing	ride on a ferry / bus / subway
go dancing	rest
write postcards	stay in the hotel

> Dear Yolene,
>   We're having a wonderful time in Mexico City. First we
> _____.
>   1
> Then _____.
>   2
> Now Maria is shopping, and I
> _____.
>   3
> See you soon!
>   Love,
>   Sylvia

2   Pretend you are taking a trip to another city. Write a postcard to a classmate. First, tell where you are. You can use:

We are having a wonderful time in . . .
. . . is a lovely / great / exciting place.
It's lovely / great / exciting here in . . .

Then tell your classmate some of the things you have done. Use the vocabulary from the box in Exercise 1. Last, tell your classmate what you are doing now.

For pronunciation exercises for Unit 3, see page 110.

4 You're a New Yorker Now

1 Dave is talking to his brother Steve. Listen to their conversation.

1

DAVE: Aren't you going to work today?

STEVE: No, we're off today. It's a school holiday, so I'm painting the living room. What are you doing today?

DAVE: I'm meeting Maria at the Empire State Building at 11:00.

2

STEVE: How was your date last night?

DAVE: Oh, we had a good time. I like Maria a lot. Say, what bus do I take to get to 34th Street and Fifth Avenue?

STEVE: The bus! You never take the bus! Where's your truck?

DAVE: It's still at the mechanic's, so today I'm taking the bus.

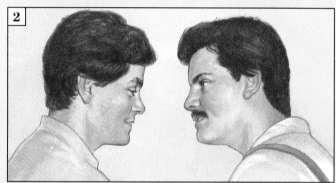

3

STEVE: Take the one that stops on the corner of St. Nicholas Avenue and 181st Street. I think it's the number 3.

DAVE: How often does it run?

STEVE: Oh, it usually comes every five minutes.

DAVE: How much is the fare?

STEVE: Don't you know the fare? You're a New Yorker now!

DAVE: But I'm a New Yorker with a truck!

STEVE: Well, it's $1, and you need exact change.

2 Answer the questions.

1. What's Steve doing today?
2. Where's Dave going?
3. Why can't Dave use his truck today?
4. How often do the buses usually run?
5. Can the bus driver make change?

3 Warm Up

Ask a classmate how often he or she does something.

A: How often do you *visit your brother?*

B: Oh, *about once a week.*

OR   I *never visit him. He always comes to my house.*

DEVELOP YOUR VOCABULARY

now and then	every other week
as often as possible	once in a blue moon
whenever I have the chance	. . .

Practice

A.

> Steve **teaches** math, but he **isn't teaching** today.
> He**'s painting** his living room.

1 Look at the pictures. Talk about what these people usually do and what they're doing today.

1. A: What does *Steve* do?
   B: *He teaches math.*
   A: Is *he teaching* today?
   B: No, *he* isn't. *He's painting his living room.*

1. Steve / teach math

2. Julie / make furniture

3. Barbara / work with computers

Can you remember what Maria and Yolanda do? Look at the pictures and talk about what they usually do and what they are doing today.

2 Ask a classmate about a friend's or relative's occupation.

A: What does *your daughter* do?
B: *She's a clerk in a department store.*
   OR   *She* works *in a department store.*
A: Is *she* working today?
B: Yes, *she* is.
   OR   No, *she's off today. She's doing errands.*

DEVELOP YOUR VOCABULARY

bookkeeper	plumber
bank teller	welder
cashier	salesperson
computer operator	. . .

> **Note:** These verbs are not usually used in the progressive form:
>
> | | |
> |---|---|
> | be | Steve **is** Dave's brother. |
> | have (= to own) | He **has** a small apartment. |
> | have to | He **has to** work hard. |
> | like | Steve **likes** New York. |
> | hate | He **hates** his apartment. |
> | need | He **needs** a bigger apartment. |
> | want (to) | However, he **doesn't want** to pay more rent. |

3 **What's the matter with Roberto? Complete the paragraph with the simple present or present progressive forms of the verbs.**

Roberto ___*isn't*___ in a good mood today. He's ___*staying*___
       _{1. be -neg.}   _{2. stay}

home today because he _____ a cold. He
                                _{3. have}

_____ some medicine, but he _____ to go
    _{4. need}   _{5. want -neg.}

outside because it _____. Yolanda _____
                       _{6. rain}   _{7. buy}

him some medicine, and she _____ him some
                             _{8. get}

magazines too. Unfortunately, Roberto _____ to go
                                       _{9. have}

out later and play at a club. He _____ to be sick,
                                _{10. hate}

and he _____ to get better soon.
      _{11. want}

B.

What's Yolanda **doing tomorrow?**	She's **working** at the festival.
Who's **playing** at the club **this weekend?**	Roberto's **playing** there **on Sunday.**

1 **Look at these pages from Yolanda's calendar. Pretend today is Friday and talk about her plans.**

A: What's Yolanda doing *tomorrow?*
B: She's *working at the Latin American Festival.*

2 Ask a classmate what he or she is doing this weekend.

A: What are you doing this weekend?

B: I'm *going swimming on Saturday,* and I'm *studying on Sunday.*

3 Complete this schedule with your activities for next week. If you do not have anything planned for a certain time, leave that space blank.

	Mon	Tues	Wed	Thurs	Fri
9:00					
10:00					
11:00					
12:00					
1:00					
2:00					
3:00					
4:00					
5:00					
6:00					
7:00					
8:00					

Now try to make plans with a classmate to do something together.

A: How would you like to *have coffee* some time next week?

B: That sounds good. When are you free?

A: Well, what are you doing next *Wednesday at 2:00?*

B: I'm *going shopping with my niece.* How about *Thursday at 4:00?*

    OR   I'm not doing anything. Let's make it for then.

A: . . .

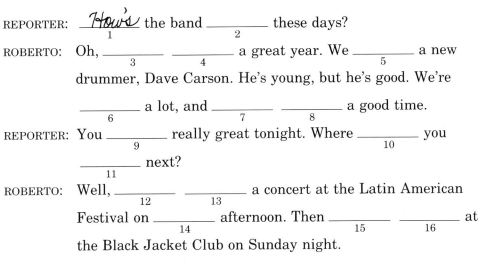

4 A reporter is asking Roberto questions about his band. Listen and complete their conversation.

REPORTER: ___*How's*___ the band _____ these days?
               1   2

ROBERTO: Oh, _____ _____ a great year. We _____ a new
                  3   4   5

drummer, Dave Carson. He's young, but he's good. We're

_____ a lot, and _____ _____ a good time.
  6   7   8

REPORTER: You _____ really great tonight. Where _____ you
               9   10

_____ next?
  11

ROBERTO: Well, _____ _____ a concert at the Latin American
              12   13

Festival on _____ afternoon. Then _____ _____ at
               14   15   16

the Black Jacket Club on Sunday night.

THE BLACK JACKET

THE
BLACK JACKET
Club
PRESENTS
LOS SANTOS
Starring Roberto
RUIZ
Sunday AT 8 P.M.

C.

Aren't you **going** to work today?	No, I'm not.	**Doesn't** Dave **play** in a band?	Yes, he does.
Isn't Dave a construction worker?	Yes, he is.	**Didn't** Dave **go** to work today?	No, he didn't.

1 Dave and Maria talked on the phone early this morning. Listen to their conversation and complete their questions.

DAVE: Can you have lunch with me today?

MARIA: *Aren't*(1) *you*(2) *going*(3) to work?

DAVE: Not today. I can't work when it's raining.

MARIA: Why? _____(4) _____(5) _____(6) in a band?

DAVE: Yes, but I'm also a construction worker.

MARIA: _____(7) _____(8) difficult work?

DAVE: Yes. But the money is good, and I like to work with my hands.

MARIA: _____(9) _____(10) _____(11) _____(12) _____(13) on tall buildings?

DAVE: Yes, sometimes. And once I almost had a bad accident.

MARIA: _____(14) _____(15) afraid?

DAVE: You bet. Now that I answered all of *your* questions, would you answer one of *mine?* _____(16) _____(17) _____(18) lunch with me today?

MARIA: I'd love to. Meet me at the Empire State Building at 11:00.

2 Pretend a classmate isn't doing what he or she usually does. Find out about it.

A: Aren't you *going to work* today?
B: No, I'm not. I *have to go to the doctor's.*

Student A can use these ideas:

taking the bus	going home after class
going to the library	going shopping
eating lunch	

Just for Fun

3 Look at each picture and write a negative question.

1. bring your umbrella? 2. hot? 3. have a hat? 4. going to work?

Life Skills

Transportation

1 Student A: You are at the World Trade Center. Find out what buses to take to these tourist sights in New York City, and ask about the fare.

1. the Empire State Building
2. Central Park
3. the United Nations

4. Radio City Music Hall
5. the Metropolitan Museum of Art
6. Grand Central Terminal

Student B: Look at the tourist brochure and answer Student A's questions.

1. A: Excuse me. What bus do I take to *the Empire State Building?*
   B: The number *1.*
   A: How much is the fare?
   B: $1, and you need exact change.

SEE NEW YORK SIGHTS BY BUS!

Remember: You need exact change ($1) for all buses.

1. The Empire State Building
   #1 to Madison Ave. and 34th St.

2. Central Park
   #10 to Central Park West and 59th St.

3. The United Nations
   #15 to 42nd St. and 1st Ave.

4. Radio City Music Hall
   #6 to 50th St. and 6th Ave.

5. The Metropolitan Museum of Art
   #1 to Madison Ave. and 81st St.

6. Grand Central Terminal
   #101 to 3rd Ave. and 42nd St.

2 Look at the bus map for part of New York City. Then complete the information below.

1. The number ___10___ bus travels south on West Broadway.
2. The number 6 bus travels north on Church Street and Avenue of the _____.
3. The number 6 bus travels _____ on Broadway.
4. The number _____ travels on Centre Street.
5. You can get two different buses at the bus stop on the corner of Fulton and _____ Streets.

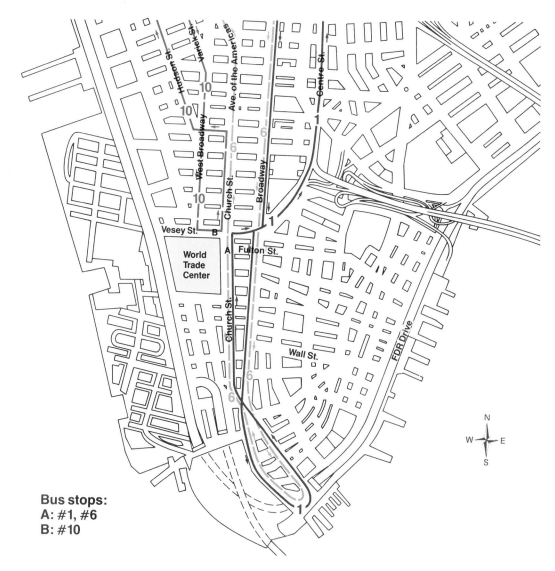

Bus stops:
A: #1, #6
B: #10

3 Student A: You are near the World Trade Center. Ask where to get these buses.

1. #6
2. #1
3. #10

Student B: Look at the map in Exercise 2 and answer Student A's questions.

A: Excuse me. Where can I get the number . . . bus?
B: Let's see. You can get it on the corner of . . . and . . .
A: Thanks.

4   **Student A: You are on a bus. Ask the bus driver where to get off for:**

1. the Empire State Building
2. Central Park
3. the United Nations
4. Radio City Music Hall
5. the Metropolitan Museum of Art
6. Grand Central Terminal

Student B: You are the bus driver. Look at the brochure on page 33 and answer Student A's questions.

1. A: Where do I get off for *the Empire State Building?*
   B: At *Madison Avenue and 34th Street.*

5   **Barbara Gorska is calling the New York City Subway and Bus Information number. She wants to go to Radio City Music Hall. Listen to the conversation and complete it.**

EMPLOYEE: New York City Transit Information.

BARBARA: Hello. I'd like to __go__ to Radio City Music Hall. What _____ do I
                      1   2

            _____ ?
               3

EMPLOYEE: _____ are you _____ from?
               4   5

BARBARA: Well, I'm standing on the _____ of First Avenue and _____ Street.
                                         6   7

EMPLOYEE: OK. You can _____ the number _____ bus.
                           8   9

BARBARA: Where can I _____ the number 27?
                          10

EMPLOYEE: There's a bus _____ at 47th Street and First Avenue.
                             11

BARBARA: And where do I _____ _____ ?
                             12   13

EMPLOYEE: At _____ Avenue.
                  14

BARBARA: OK. Thank you very much.

EMPLOYEE: You're welcome. Goodbye.

Now practice the conversation with a classmate. Use information about your city or town.

ON YOUR OWN
Discuss these questions with your classmates.

1 What types of transportation do you use? What do you think is good or bad about them?

2 Do you think the transportation system in New York is very different from the transportation system in your country? If so, how is it different?

For pronunciation exercises for Unit 4, see page 111.

REVIEW 2

1 Ask questions about Janet Garvey.

1. A: _When did Janet Garvey go to jail_?
   B: She went to jail two years ago.
2. A: _____?
   B: Because she robbed a store.
3. A: _____?
   B: She stole money and jewelry.
4. A: _____?
   B: Two hundred dollars.

5. A: _____?
   B: No, she didn't have a gun.
6. A: _____?
   B: Only one year. Then she escaped.
7. A: _____?
   B: No, they didn't. The police are still looking for her.

2 Complete these sentences with *could* or *couldn't*.

1. Yolanda _couldn't_ catch the thief. She escaped.
2. Dave _____ go to the Tina Turner concert. He didn't have the money for a ticket.
3. Dave thought Maria was lucky because she _____ see Tina Turner.

4. When Maria was a child, she _____ speak a little English. She learned it in Poland.
5. Yolanda's son _____ pass his last math test. He has to study more.
6. Barbara _____ see what was happening on the street, so she asked her brother to tell her.

3 Look at the activities in the box. Check the things you could do when you were a child. Then write six sentences about what you *could* and *couldn't* do.

| speak English | jump rope | swim |
| play the piano | ride a bike | cook |

4 Ask questions about Yolanda. Use the words in parentheses.

1. A: _What's Yolanda doing_? (do)
   B: She's working.
2. A: _____? (work)
   B: In the living room.
3. A: _____? (make)
   B: A new necklace.
4. A: _____? (think about)
   B: Janet Garvey.

5 Look at the chart about Dave. Then complete the questions and answer them. Use *still* or *not . . . anymore*.

1. A: Is Dave still _living_ in Chicago?
   B: _No. He isn't living there anymore_.
2. A: Is he still _____ a car?
   B: _____.
3. A: Is he still _____ singing?
   B: _____.
4. A: Is he still _____ Susan?
   B: _____.
5. A: Is he still _____ baseball?
   B: _____.

Now	Five years ago
lives in New York	lived in Chicago
studies singing	studied singing
drives a truck	drove a car
dates Maria	dated Susan
plays baseball	played baseball

6 Complete this paragraph with the simple present or present progressive form of the verbs.

Barbara Gorska ___*is*___ a computer programmer. Right now, she *'s sitting* at her desk.
1. be   2. sit

She _____ a good job at a big company. She always _____ very hard. This week
3. have   4. work

she _____ on a new project and _____ to stay late every night. On weekends she
5. work   6. have

often _____ to discos with friends. She _____ music a lot. She _____ a musical
7. go   8. like   9. play *-neg.*

instrument, but she _____ to learn. She _____ for a piano teacher to give her
10. want   11. look

lessons. Maybe Dave _____ one.
12. know

7 Complete these questions. Then answer them with your own information.

1. Where ___*are*___ you ___*eating*___ tomorrow
                   eat
   night?

2. What _____ you _____ next weekend?
                do

3. When _____ your friend _____ to see you?
                        come

4. Who _____ _____ home next year?
             go

5. When _____ we _____ class today?
                leave

8 Ask negative questions about Steve and Dave. Use the words in parentheses.

1. Steve is staying home today.   (working)

Isn't he working?

2. Steve is painting the kitchen.   (living room)
3. Dave has a car.   (truck)
4. Dave is taking the train today.   (bus)
5. The fare is 90¢.   ($1.00)
6. Dave had a date with Susan last night.   (Maria)
7. Steve teaches English.   (math)

Just for Fun

9 Complete this crossword puzzle.

Across
1. Garvey's first name
4. Please come _____ time.
6. _____ are you leaving?
8. nine + one = _____
9. past of *can*
11. English, for example
14. *I am* (contraction)
15. past of *eat*
16. past of *get*

Down
1. Garvey spent one year there
2. a negative word
3. Turner's first name
4. _____, no!
5. a piece of jewelry
6. past of *go*
7. _____, I didn't.
10. a musical instrument
12. Maria is Dave's _____ friend.
13. opposite of *west*

1 Dave and Maria are walking to Central Park. Listen to their conversation.

1

MARIA: When did you come to New York?

DAVE: My brother got a job here a few years ago. I came to visit him and decided to stay. What about you?

MARIA: Well, my family came here from Poland when I was six. We lived in the East Village before we moved to West 76th Street.

DAVE: I'm sure you had a hard time when you first arrived.

MARIA: Yeah. I really did. I felt so out of place.

2

DAVE: Did you study art or did you teach yourself?

MARIA: I studied art and design in night school. I want to work for a fashion designer, but it's hard to find a job.

DAVE: I know what you mean. I'd like to play in a band full time.

3

MARIA: Where would you like to have lunch?

DAVE: Well, uh . . . I don't know.

REPORTER: Excuse me, ma'am. I'm a reporter from the magazine *Around New York,* and I'd like to ask you some questions for a survey.

MARIA: We have time, Dave, don't we?

DAVE: Sure. Go ahead.

2 Answer the questions.

1. Where is Maria from?
2. What kind of job does Maria want?
3. What would Dave like to do?
4. Who wants to ask Maria some questions?

3 Warm Up

Talk about what you would like to do.

A: What kind of job would you like to have?

B: I'd like to be *an actor. I love the theater.*

OR   I'd like to *work for a newspaper. It's exciting.*

OR   I like my job. I don't want to change it.

DEVELOP YOUR VOCABULARY

own *a grocery store*
be *an engineer*
get *a full-time job as a lab technician*
. . .

Practice

A.

I	plan to be decided to become	a fashion designer.

Other verbs that follow this pattern:		
begin	hope	promise
expect	like	remember
forget	love	want
hate	need	

1 Maria answered the reporter's questions. Listen to their conversation and make notes about what Maria tells the reporter.

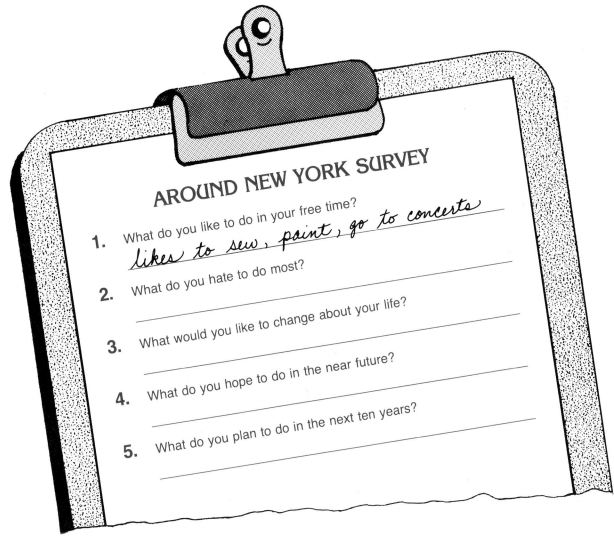

AROUND NEW YORK SURVEY

1. What do you like to do in your free time?
   likes to sew, paint, go to concerts

2. What do you hate to do most?

3. What would you like to change about your life?

4. What do you hope to do in the near future?

5. What do you plan to do in the next ten years?

2 Now look at the survey form and talk about Maria like this:

Maria likes to sew, paint and go to concerts.

3 Interview several classmates using the questions in Exercise 1. Take notes and report back to the class.

4 Find out what activities a classmate likes and dislikes.

A: Do you like to *dance?*

B: Yes, but I hate to *go to discos.*
   OR   No, I hate to *dance,* but I love to *listen to music.*

B.

When I was six, I came to the U.S.	OR	I came to the U.S. **when I was six.**
Before we moved to West 76th Street, I lived in the East Village.	OR	I lived in the East Village **before we moved to West 76th Street.**
After I finished high school, I started to work.	OR	I started to work **after I finished high school.**

1 Look at this information about Maria's life. Then combine the sentences below with the words in parentheses. Use a comma when necessary.

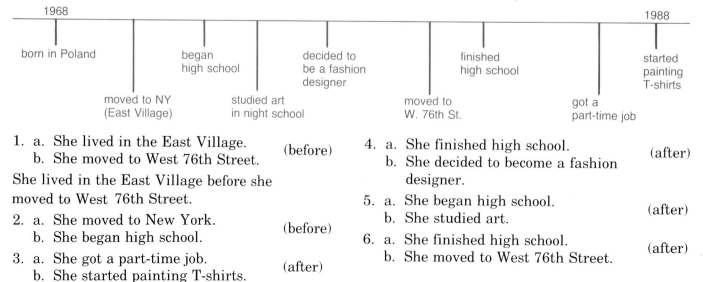

1. a. She lived in the East Village.
   b. She moved to West 76th Street.   (before)

She lived in the East Village before she moved to West 76th Street.

2. a. She moved to New York.
   b. She began high school.   (before)

3. a. She got a part-time job.
   b. She started painting T-shirts.   (after)

4. a. She finished high school.
   b. She decided to become a fashion designer.   (after)

5. a. She began high school.
   b. She studied art.   (after)

6. a. She finished high school.
   b. She moved to West 76th Street.   (after)

2 Yolanda's son, Ricky, has to write a composition about a famous immigrant to the United States. Listen to his conversation with his mother and choose the correct information from the box to fill in the blanks.

baseball player	China
architect	Greece
movie producer	Puerto Rico

1.
NAME *Roberto Clemente*

PLACE OF BIRTH _____

OCCUPATION _____

2.
NAME *I. M. Pei*

PLACE OF BIRTH _____

OCCUPATION _____

3.
NAME *Spyros Skouras*

PLACE OF BIRTH _____

OCCUPATION _____

3 Now read the composition that Ricky wrote about his father and complete it with the correct words.

Roberto Ruiz was born in Cuba. **When** he was very young, he always liked
1. Before / When
to listen to music. There were no musical instruments at home, but he always
smiled _____ his mother sang or turned on the radio. _____ he started
2. after / when   3. After / Before
school, he learned to play the piano.
_____ he studied for only a few months, he could play very well. His
4. After / Before
teacher recommended a special music school. Unfortunately, Roberto never had the
opportunity to go there. _____ his classes began, his family had to leave Cuba.
5. After / Before
     This was a hard time for Roberto. He studied English in Cuba _____ he
6. after / before
came to the United States, but _____ he arrived he didn't speak very well. He
7. before / when
felt out of place, and his music became his life. He always practiced
_____ he was unhappy. He studied hard, and he also learned to play the
8. after / when
trombone, the guitar and the drums. Today Roberto Ruiz is a well-known bandleader
in New York.

4   Ask a classmate questions about his or her life.

A: How did you feel when you first arrived here?
B: *Frightened and homesick.*

**You can use these suggestions or
your own ideas:**

How / feel / when / first arrived here
Where / live / before / came here
What / do / before / came here
What / do / after / arrived
speak English / when / first arrived
feel nervous / before / started this class

DEVELOP YOUR VOCABULARY

terrified	excited
nervous	thrilled
out of place	optimistic
disappointed	. . .

C.

You're Polish,	**aren't you?**
He wasn't born in the United States,	**was he?**
She's living with her family,	**isn't she?**
They live in New York now,	**don't they?**
You didn't speak English at home,	**did you?**
Roberto couldn't speak English,	**could he?**

Exception: **I'm** early, **aren't I?**

1   You can ask tag questions to check information you think is true. Complete the questions and answer them. Check your answers with the information on pages 40 and 41.

1. A: Spyros Skouras was a famous movie producer, _wasn't he_?
    B: Yes, he was.

2. Roberto Clemente wasn't born in Cuba, _____?

3. I. M. Pei is Chinese, _____?

4. Roberto Ruiz started music lessons in Cuba, _____?

5. Roberto Clemente was a famous basketball player, _____?

6. Spyros Skouras didn't come from Greece, _____?

7. Roberto Ruiz is living in New York today, _____?

8. When he was young, Roberto could play the piano, _____?

9. Maria Gorska started high school before she came to New York, _____?

2 What do you know about your classmate's life?

A: You were born in *Hong Kong*, weren't you?
B: Yes, I was.   OR   No, I was born in
Taiwan.

You can use these suggestions or your own ideas:

born / *Hong Kong*	live / *in Brooklyn*
speak / *French*	worked / ~~as a~~
have / *two sisters*	

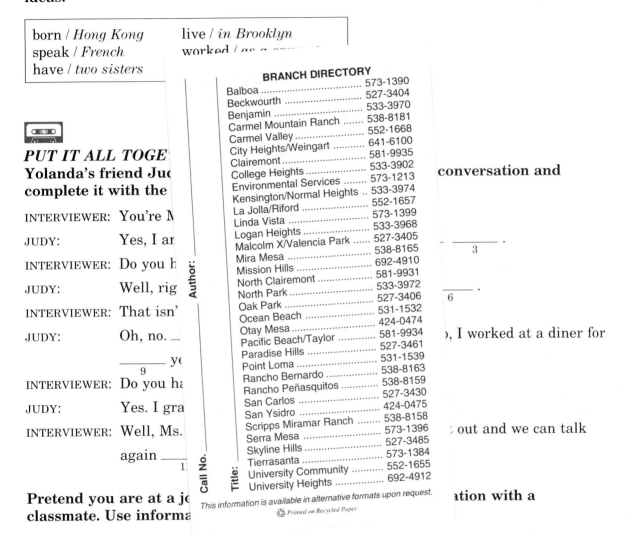

PUT IT ALL TOGE...
Yolanda's friend Ju... conversation and complete it with the...

INTERVIEWER: You're M...

JUDY: Yes, I a...

INTERVIEWER: Do you h...

JUDY: Well, rig...

INTERVIEWER: That isn'...

JUDY: Oh, no. _____ ..., I worked at a diner for
_____ ye...
9

INTERVIEWER: Do you ha...

JUDY: Yes. I gra...

INTERVIEWER: Well, Ms. ... out and we can talk
again _____
1...

Pretend you are at a j... ...ation with a classmate. Use informa...

BRANCH DIRECTORY

Balboa	573-1390
Beckwourth	527-3404
Benjamin	533-3970
Carmel Mountain Ranch	538-8181
Carmel Valley	552-1668
City Heights/Weingart	641-6100
Clairemont	581-9935
College Heights	533-3902
Environmental Services	573-1213
Kensington/Normal Heights	533-3974
La Jolla/Riford	552-1657
Linda Vista	573-1399
Logan Heights	533-3968
Malcolm X/Valencia Park	527-3405
Mira Mesa	538-8165
Mission Hills	692-4910
North Clairemont	581-9931
North Park	533-3972
Oak Park	527-3406
Ocean Beach	531-1532
Otay Mesa	424-0474
Pacific Beach/Taylor	581-9934
Paradise Hills	527-3461
Point Loma	531-1539
Rancho Bernardo	538-8163
Rancho Peñasquitos	538-8159
San Carlos	527-3430
San Ysidro	424-0475
Scripps Miramar Ranch	538-8158
Serra Mesa	573-1396
Skyline Hills	527-3485
Tierrasanta	573-1384
University Community	552-1655
University Heights	692-4912

This information is available in alternative formats upon request.
Printed on Recycled Paper

Author: *Call No.* *Title:*

ON YOUR OWN
Think about how Maria felt when she moved to New York. Then discuss these questions with your classmates.

Did you ever move to a new city or country?
How did you feel when you moved? Did you feel
comfortable or out of place? Was it easy or
difficult to make friends? To find a job? A place
to live?

Reading

When Good Luck Means Hard Work

Spyros Skouras was born on a poor farm in Greece in 1893. In 1942, he became the president of 20th Century-Fox, an important movie studio.
(5) Between 1893 and 1942, Skouras learned to change bad luck to good luck. His secret? Hard work and a great personality.

When Spyros was still a boy, the
(10) Skouras farm failed and Spyros's older brother Charles came to America. In 1910, Charles sent Spyros the money to join him in St. Louis. There, Spyros worked as a waiter twelve hours a day
(15) in a hotel and studied English and law at night. Within a year, Charles and Spyros sent for their younger brother George.

The three brothers had great
(20) dreams. In 1913, they bought their first movie theater. Soon after, they bought another one, and before long they owned part of every theater in St. Louis. By 1925, the Skouras brothers
(25) were famous in the movie industry.

Older brother Charles was the head of the family, but Spyros spoke for the Skouras brothers in business deals. Someone said of Spyros in those days,
(30) "No one could understand him, but everybody believed him." People trusted Spyros's warm personality and optimism, so his poor English did not matter much.

(35) This optimism helped Spyros. In 1929, the United States stock market crashed. The Skouras brothers lost almost everything, but bad luck only made Spyros more ambitious. After
(40) the crash, the brothers bought more theaters and built a new movie fortune. This time they were even more successful, and in 1942, 20th Century-Fox made Spyros its president.

1 Comprehension. Complete the sentences.

1. The Skouras brothers were born in
   a. St. Louis.
   b. Greece.
   c. Chicago.

2. When he first came to America, Spyros
   a. studied all day and worked at night.
   b. worked all day and studied at night.
   c. spent all his time at the movies.

3. Spyros spoke for the family in business deals because
   a. he spoke excellent English.
   b. Charles was the older brother.
   c. people trusted him.

4. After the stock market crash, Spyros
   a. returned to Greece.
   b. worked at a hotel.
   c. made more money in the movie business.

2 Vocabulary building. Complete the sentences with words from the story.

fortune	ambitious	optimism	personality

1. The Skouras brothers were _ambitious_. They wanted great success in the movie industry.

2. Spyros's warm _____ helped people to trust him.

3. The Skouras brothers lost all their money in the 1929 stock market crash, but soon made a new _____.

4. Spyros Skouras believed things would turn out well. He had a lot of _____.

3 Understanding the order of events. Match the date and the event.

1. _c_ 1893   a. The Skouras brothers lost most of their money.

2. ____ 1910   b. Spyros Skouras became president of a movie studio.

3. ____ 1925   c. Spyros Skouras was born in Greece.

4. ____ 1929   d. Spyros came to St. Louis.

5. ____ 1942   e. The Skouras brothers were famous in the movie industry.

Writing

Skill: Organizing paragraphs using time words—*when, during* and *after*
Task: Writing about a job

When you look for a job, you often have to write about other jobs you have had.
The words *when, during* and *after* can help you describe a job you had in the past.

> **Note:** Use *during* when you talk about a period of time.
> *During the summer, I worked as a waitress.*

1 Think of a job you once had. It can be a job you were paid for or work you
   did for your school or family. Then answer the questions about the job.
   Follow the examples.

QUESTIONS	EXAMPLE 1	EXAMPLE 2
When did you have this job? (Use *when, during* or *in*.)	When I was 13,	During the summer of 1980, OR In 1980,
What was the job?	I took my younger brother to school every day.	I was a crime reporter.
Where was the job?	We lived in Ghana, and our school was a mile from our house.	I worked for the *China Daily News* in Taipei.
What did you do on this job? (Use *first, then* and *after*.)	First I dressed my brother. Then I walked him to school. We crossed a lot of busy streets on the way. After we got to school, I took him to his classroom.	First I got my assignment* from my editor. Then I went to the scene of the crime. I interviewed people and talked to the police. After I talked to everyone, I went back to the office and wrote my story.
What did you learn on this job? (Begin or end your answer with *on this job*.)	On this job, I learned to take care of a young child.	I learned how to write crime news on this job.

*A reporter's *assignment* is his or her job for that day.

2 Now write your answer to these questions as a paragraph of connected
   sentences. Be sure to indent the first line of your paragraph.

EXAMPLE 1:
    When I was 13, I took my younger brother to school every day. We lived in Ghana, and our school was a mile from our house. First I dressed my brother. Then I walked him to school. We crossed a lot of busy streets on the way. After we got to school, I took him to his classroom. On this job, I learned to take care of a young child.

EXAMPLE 2:
    During the summer of 1980, I was a crime reporter. I worked for the *China Daily News* in Taipei. First I got my assignment from my editor. Then I went to the scene of the crime. I interviewed people and talked to the police. After I talked to everyone, I went back to the office and wrote my story. I learned how to write crime news on this job.

For pronunciation exercises for Unit 5, see page 111.

A Surprise Party

1 Steve and his wife, Julie, are at a coffee shop. Listen to their conversation.

1

WAITRESS: What would you like?

STEVE: I'd like some coffee and a piece of apple pie.

JULIE: Let's see. Oh, just coffee for me, thank you. Steve, have you got any ideas for Dave's birthday?

STEVE: Well, we can take him out to dinner.

JULIE: We do that every year. I know. Let's have a surprise party for him.

STEVE: That's a great idea. He loves surprises.

2

JULIE: Let's have a barbecue. We can make hamburgers and hot dogs.

STEVE: Hmm. That's not a bad idea. We can buy some snacks like potato chips and pretzels. And you can make your famous baked beans.

JULIE: Great! Let's go. We've got a lot of work to do.

STEVE: Excuse me, miss. Can we have the check, please?

3

JULIE: We have to invite people soon. We haven't got much time.

STEVE: We can start calling people tonight.

JULIE: Oh, what about a birthday cake?

STEVE: Why don't we order one right now?

2 Answer these questions with the correct name: *Dave, Julie* or *Steve*.

Who . . .

1. is having a birthday?
2. can make baked beans?
3. likes surprises?
4. asked for the check?

3 Warm Up

Plan a party for someone.

A: Let's have *an anniversary* party for *Carol and Bill*.

B: That's a good idea. We can have *Italian* food.

A: Yeah. I can make my famous *lasagna*.

DEVELOP YOUR VOCABULARY

housewarming party   graduation party
going away party   engagement party

Chinese—beef and broccoli
Indian—curry
Mexican—tacos

Practice

A.

Count nouns		Noncount nouns
We have **a** birthday cake. We have **some** paper plates.		We have **some** fruit.
We don't have	**a** birthday cake. **any** paper plates.	We don't have **any** fruit.
Do you have	**a** birthday cake? **any** paper plates?	Do you have **any** fruit?

1 Here is a list of things Steve and Julie need for the party.

ground meat
hot dogs
ketchup
mustard
hamburger buns
hot dog buns
lettuce
pickles
onions
bacon

brown sugar
potato chips
pretzels
fruit
birthday cake

decorations
napkins
paper plates
paper tablecloth
plastic cups
plastic silverware
table
folding chairs
charcoal

lighter fluid
barbecue grill

Look at the items on the list. Decide which nouns are count and which nouns are noncount.

Count	Noncount
hot dogs	*ground meat*
. . .	. . .

2 Now listen to Steve and Julie's conversation and look at their list. Check the items they already have.

3 Look at the list and ask and answer questions like these:

A: Do they have *any ketchup?*
B: Yes, they do.
A: Do they have *a barbecue grill?*
B: No, they don't.

4 Julie is talking to her mother on the telephone. Read their conversation and complete it with _some_, _any_ or _a_.

JULIE: Mom, this is Julie. Do you have _any_ folding chairs? We're having a party for Dave, and we need some.

MOTHER: Sure. Do you need anything else?

JULIE: Well, we don't have _____ large table.
2

MOTHER: I can lend you one. Is that all?

JULIE: Well, we also need _____ barbecue grill and _____ charcoal.
3 4

MOTHER: OK. You can borrow my grill, and I have some charcoal. I have _____ plastic silverware and _____ paper tablecloth too. Do you need those?
5 6

JULIE: Yes, we do. And Mom . . .

MOTHER: Yes?

JULIE: Well . . . uh . . . Could we have the party at your house?

MOTHER: Sure.

B.

I've He's	**got**	some	soda.
They **haven't**		any	

Have you	**got**	any soda?	Yes, I **do.**
Has he			No, he **doesn't.**

I have got = I've got
he has got = he's got

1 With another classmate, make a list of the food you would like to serve at a party. Now find out what you have and what you need to buy.

A: Have you got any _soda?_
B: Yes, I do. We don't need to buy any.
A: Have you got any _cheese?_
B: No, I don't. We need to buy some.

2 Look at the list and decide what to get Dave for his birthday.

A: What should we get Dave for his birthday?
B: He likes _sports._ How about _a bowling ball?_
A: No, he's got _a bowling ball._ Let's get something different.
B: Like what?
A: How about _a tennis racket?_
B: That's a good idea. He hasn't got _a tennis racket._

DAVE'S GOT	DAVE HASN'T GOT
Sports	
bowling ball baseball glove	tennis racket skis football golf balls
Photography	
photo album camera bag	books on photography tripod
Camping	
sleeping bag first-aid kit	lantern hiking boots grill

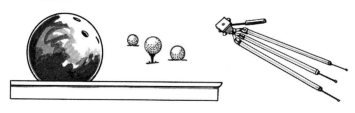

C.

Count	Noncount
How many onions do we need?	**How much** sugar do we need?
We need **two pounds of** onions.	We need **three cups of** sugar.

1 **Julie's cousin Tina wants Julie's recipe for baked beans. Listen to their conversation and complete the recipe.**

RECIPE

BAKED BEANS AND FRUIT

Two 16–ounce _Cans_ of baked beans
_____
1

¼ _____ of bacon
2

_____ large onion
3

_____ apples
4

_____ orange
5

_____ _____ of brown sugar
6   7

Mix all the ingredients together except the bacon. Put the mixture in a baking dish. Place the bacon in strips across the top. Bake at 300°F (about 150°C) for 1½ hours.

2 **The recipe is enough for eight people, but twenty-four people are coming to Steve and Julie's party. Look at the recipe again and change the quantities. Ask and answer questions like this:**

A: How many *cans of baked beans* do we need?
B: *Six 16-ounce cans.*
A: How much *bacon* do we need?
B: . . .

Just for Fun

3 **Look at the pictures.**

| bottle | can | jar | box | carton | bag |

How can you buy these foods?

flour	jelly	potatoes	milk
juice	tomato sauce	coffee	oil
spaghetti	cookies	soda	rice

A: You can buy a *bag of flour.*
B: You can buy a *box of flour* too.

D.

Count	Noncount
(not) **many** hours	not **much** time
a few dollars	**a little** money
a lot of chairs	**a lot of** furniture

> **Note:** You usually use *much* in negative statements and questions only.

1 Look at the words below. Decide which ones are count nouns and which ones are noncount nouns.

time	hour	money	dollar	furniture	chair
trouble	problem	fun	food	hamburger	people

Count

_____ _____

_____ _____

. . .   . . .

Noncount

_____ _____

_____ _____

. . .   . . .

2 Dave is thanking Julie and Steve for the party. Complete their conversation with *much, many, a few* or *a little*. Add *s* or *es* to the count nouns only.

DAVE: Thanks a lot for the party. I had a lot of fun. I didn't know I had so __*many*__ friend*s*.
1. much / many

JULIE: I'm glad you enjoyed it. It really wasn't _____ trouble__. We didn't have
2. much / many

_____ problem __, and it only took us _____ hour__.
3. much / many   4. a few / a little

DAVE: You certainly made a lot of food, but there are only _____ hamburger__
5. a few / a little

and _____ cake__ left. I hope you didn't spend _____ money__.
6. a few / a little   7. much / many

STEVE: Don't worry. It wasn't expensive. We didn't spend _____ money__ at all.
8. much / many

JULIE: You got some nice presents, Dave.

DAVE: Yeah, I sure did. There were a lot of people here too. Well, let's start to clean up.

STEVE: Don't worry about that. There aren't _____ dish__. Sit down and relax!
9. much / many

3 Talk about a good party you went to recently.

A: I went to *a great* party *last night.*
B: *Were* there a lot of *interesting people?*
A: Yes, and there *was* a lot of *good food* too.
    OR   No, but there *was* a lot of *good food.*

Now talk about a bad party.

A: I went to *an awful* party *last week.*
B: Why was it *awful? Were* there a lot of *unfriendly people?*
A: Yes, and there *was* a lot of *loud music* too.
    OR   No, but there *was* a lot of *loud music.*

You can use these ideas:

boring people	noise
dancing	smoke
interesting conversation	

Life Skills

Food and restaurants

1 Look at the pictures of the menu specials at Sam's Diner. Then talk about the specials like this:

A: What does the *spaghetti dinner* come with?

B: It comes with *salad, soda* and *dessert.*

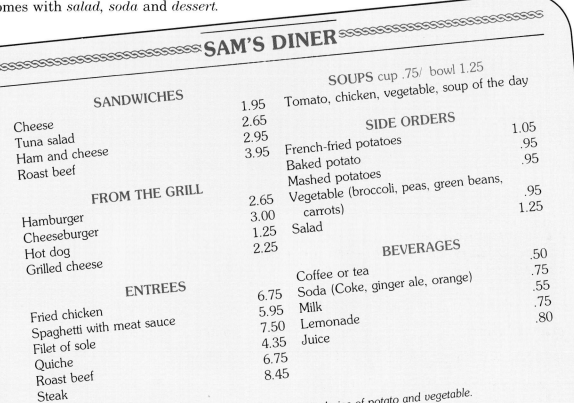

SAM'S DINER

SANDWICHES

Cheese	1.95
Tuna salad	2.65
Ham and cheese	2.95
Roast beef	3.95

FROM THE GRILL

Hamburger	2.65
Cheeseburger	3.00
Hot dog	1.25
Grilled cheese	2.25

ENTREES

Fried chicken	6.75
Spaghetti with meat sauce	5.95
Filet of sole	7.50
Quiche	4.35
Roast beef	6.75
Steak	8.45

SOUPS cup .75/ bowl 1.25

Tomato, chicken, vegetable, soup of the day

SIDE ORDERS

French-fried potatoes	1.05
Baked potato	.95
Mashed potatoes	.95
Vegetable (broccoli, peas, green beans, carrots)	.95
Salad	1.25

BEVERAGES

Coffee or tea	.50
Soda (Coke, ginger ale, orange)	.75
Milk	.55
Lemonade	.75
Juice	.80

All entrées except spaghetti served with choice of potato and vegetable.

SPECIAL $6.95   Spaghetti Dinner

spaghetti, salad, soda, chocolate cake

SPECIAL $5.65   Quiche Lunch

quiche, baked potato, green beans, cup of coffee

Ham and Cheese Special $3.60

ham and cheese sandwich, french fries, glass of milk

SPECIAL $9.25   Filet of Sole Dinner

filet of sole, mashed potatoes, broccoli, cup of tea

Cheeseburger Special $5.00

cheeseburger, lemonade, apple pie

Hot Dog Special $2.95

hot dog, peas, milk, ice cream

2 You have $8.00. Which meals can you order from the menu on page 51?

1. a grilled cheese sandwich and a soda
2. the fried chicken, a baked potato and coffee
3. the spaghetti special
4. a tuna salad sandwich and a salad
5. the quiche lunch special
6. the filet of sole and a cup of the soup of the day

3 Look back at the menu and order.

WAITER: Are you ready to order?
CUSTOMER: Yes, I'd like *a roast beef sandwich.*
WAITER: Anything to drink?
CUSTOMER: Yes. I'll have *a cup of tea.*

Just for Fun

4 Look at the two pictures. List the five things missing in the second picture and ask the waiter for them.

CUSTOMER: Excuse me. Could I have *some sugar?*
WAITER: Sure.

5 Pretend the waiter forgot to bring something you ordered. Ask for it.

CUSTOMER: Excuse me, sir. I ordered *a cup of tea.*
WAITER: Oh, sorry, I'll get you *one* right away.

> **Note:** a cup of tea → *one*
> carrots → *some*

6 Student A (Waiter): Look at the list of today's desserts and answer the customer's questions.

   Student B (Customer): Find out what kind of desserts the restaurant has.

WAITER: Would you like anything for dessert?
CUSTOMER: Yes. What kind of *pie* do you have?
WAITER: . . . , . . . , . . . and . . .
CUSTOMER: I'll have the . . .

DESSERT MENU

Today's Ice Cream
chocolate, strawberry, vanilla, lemon sherbet

Today's Cake
chocolate, strawberry, shortcake, lemon

Today's Pie
apple, chocolate cream, cherry, lemon meringue

7 Dictation

Barbara Gorska is ordering dinner. Listen to the conversation. Then listen again and complete it.

WAITRESS: _____?
1

BARBARA: Yes. I'll have the roast beef.

WAITRESS: _____?
2

BARBARA: The mashed potatoes. And I get a vegetable too, don't I?

WAITRESS: _____?
3

BARBARA: I'll have the carrots.

WAITRESS: _____?
4

BARBARA: A glass of milk, please. Oh, and can I have the check now?

WAITRESS: _____ .
5

Now pretend you are ordering in a restaurant. Use the menu on page 51.

For Your Information

Tipping

In the United States and Canada, it is usual to leave your waiter or waitress a tip— extra money for service. Before leaving the restaurant, you leave the tip on the table. Most people leave about 15% of the total bill.

8 Look at Barbara's check. Then complete the sentences with the correct word.

1. Barbara has to pay ___#7.90___ .
   $7.30 / $7.90
2. Barbara had a roast beef _____ .
   dinner / sandwich
3. The tax is _____ .
   $.55 / $.60
4. The check _____ correct.
   is / isn't
5. The beverage _____ with the entrée.
   comes / doesn't come
6. Barbara is probably going to leave a tip of

   _____ .
   $.60 / $1.20

roast beef	6	75
mashed potatoes		
carrots		
milk		55
Subtotal	7	30
Tax		60
TOTAL	7	90

ON YOUR OWN

Think about Dave's surprise party. Then discuss these questions with your classmates.

1 How do you like to celebrate your birthday? What do you think about surprise parties? Did you ever go to one or have one?

2 What kinds of parties do people give in your country? Do they give surprise parties?

For pronunciation exercises for Unit 6, see page 111.

REVIEW 3 _____

1 Write questions with these words.

1. Where / want / eat dinner

Where do you want to eat dinner?

2. What / forget / do last week
3. Where / plan / be next year at this time

4. Who / expect / see tomorrow
5. What / like / drink at breakfast
6. When / decide / come to this class
7. Why / need / study English

Now write answers to the questions in Exercise 1.

2 Look at the information about Dave Carson. Then complete the sentences about Dave with *when, before* or *after*.

1964   **1988**

| born in Chicago | went to grade school and studied piano | on high school baseball team | got a car | graduated from high school | moved to New York | got a job in construction | got a truck | joined Roberto Ruiz's band | met Maria |

1. __Before__ Dave moved to New York, he lived in Chicago.
2. He studied the piano _____ he was in grade school.
3. _____ he was in high school, he played baseball.
4. _____ he graduated from high school, he got a car.

5. _____ he moved to New York, he graduated from high school.
6. _____ he got a job in construction, he bought a truck.
7. Dave met Maria _____ he joined Roberto's band.

3 Match the sentences in column A with the tag questions in column B.

A	B
1. _c_ Dave has a brother,	a. does he?
2. ____ Maria comes from Poland,	b. didn't she?
3. ____ The Empire State building isn't in Chicago,	c. doesn't he?
4. ____ Dave doesn't speak Polish,	d. aren't I?
5. ____ Roberto Ruiz wasn't born in the United States,	e. was he?
6. ____ I'm on time,	f. is it?
7. ____ Judy went for a job interview,	g. doesn't she?
8. ____ Dave had a birthday party,	h. did they?
9. ____ They didn't have a cake for Dave,	i. didn't he?

Now answer the questions in Exercise 3.

1. Yes, he does.

4 Barbara Gorska met John at Dave's party. Read their conversation and complete it with *some, any* or *a(n)*.

JOHN: Do you have _any_ brothers or sisters, Barbara?
                                  1

BARBARA: Yes, I have _____ sister and two brothers. What about you?
                              2

JOHN: No, I don't have _____ brothers or sisters. I'm _____ only child. Oh, hi, Dave.
                                   3   4

54

DAVE: Hi. Would you two like _____ cup of coffee?
5

JOHN: Yes. That sounds good. I think I'll have _____ with _____ piece of birthday
6   7

cake. What about you, Barbara?

BARBARA: Well, I don't think I want _____ coffee now, but I'd love _____ cake, thanks.
8   9

5 Ask questions with *How many* or *How much*.

1. A: Ricky ate a lot of hot dogs.
   B: *How many did he eat* ?
2. A: Yolanda drank a lot of coffee.
   B: _____?
3. A: Steve and Julie made a lot of food.
   B: _____?

4. A: Barbara met a lot of people.
   B: _____?
5. A: Dave took a lot of pictures.
   B: _____?
6. A: Julie used a lot of charcoal.
   B: _____?

6 Barbara and Maria are talking about the party. Complete their conversation.

MARIA: Did you have a good time at Dave's party?

BARBARA: Yes. It was really *a lot of* fun. How about you?
                            1. a lot of / a little

MARIA: Well, at first I didn't know _____ people, but then I met
                                    2. many / much

_____ interesting ones.
3. a little / a few

BARBARA: There sure was _____ good food, wasn't there?
                        4. much / a lot of

MARIA: Yes. I didn't eat _____ hamburgers or hot dogs, but I sure
                        5. many / a few

had _____ cake!
    6. a little / a lot of

7 Rewrite these sentences. Use *have got*.

1. Do you have any brothers or sisters?

Have you got any brothers or sisters?

2. Barbara has a sister and two brothers.

3. John doesn't have any sisters or brothers.
4. Does Dave have any brothers?
5. Does Dave have a full-time job?
6. Dave has a truck, but he doesn't have a car.

Now answer questions 1, 4 and 5. Use *have got*.

Just for Fun

8 Unscramble the letters in these words. Then decide if the word is a count or noncount noun.

	count	noncount
	party	

1. taypr
2. odof
3. eloppe
4. myone
5. acemar
6. thybriad

1 Dave's father called him on the phone. Listen to their conversation.

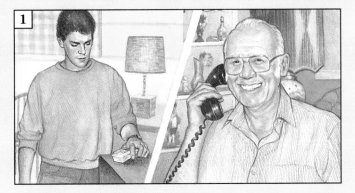

1

MR. CARSON: Hi, Dave.

DAVE: Oh, hi, Dad. How are you doing?

MR. CARSON: Well, I've got some great news.

DAVE: Oh, did you get a promotion at work?

MR. CARSON: No. I quit my job.

DAVE: You what?

MR. CARSON: I quit my job, and I'm not going to look for a new one.

DAVE: Why? What happened?

MR. CARSON: I just won the lottery.

DAVE: You're kidding!

MR. CARSON: No, I won two million dollars.

2

DAVE: Two million dollars! That's terrific! What are you going to do?

MR. CARSON: Well, first your mother and I are going to take a trip around the world.

DAVE: Dad, that's fantastic. When are you going to leave?

MR. CARSON: Soon. Maybe this month.

3

DAVE: Is Mom going to quit her job too?

MR. CARSON: She's not sure. She might go back to work after our trip.

DAVE: Two million dollars! I can't believe it!

MR. CARSON: I know. I can't either.

2 Answer the questions.

1. Was Dave surprised at his father's news?
2. Did Mr. Carson quit his job because he got a new one?
3. What are the Carsons going to do first?
4. Is Mrs. Carson going to get another job?

3 Warm Up

Pretend you just got great news. Tell a friend.

A: Guess what! I just *got a new job!*

B: That's *terrific.* Let's go celebrate!

A: OK. Why don't we *go have lunch at the Rose Café?*

DEVELOP YOUR VOCABULARY

became a grandparent
passed the *TOEFL* test
got { my green card
{ my driver's license
. . .

Practice

A.

What are you	going to do?	I'm (not) We're (not)	going to quit.
What's she		She's (not)	

Are	you they	going to travel?	Yes,	I am.		No,	I'm not.	
				we they	are.		we they	aren't.
Is he				he is.			he isn't.	

1   A reporter interviewed Mr. and Mrs. Carson and wrote this article. Complete the article with the correct form of *be going to* and the verb.

CHICAGO COUPLE WINS LOTTERY

Mr. and Mrs. Gregory Carson <u>are going to get</u> a check for
　　　　　　　　　　　　　　　　　　　1. get
$2 million today because they just won the Illinois State Lottery. Mr.
Carson, 55, said that he read the winning numbers in the newspaper
and he immediately called his wife, Martha, 53. He then quit his job at
Anderson Electronics. "Why work? I'm rich," said Carson. However,
Martha Carson, who works at Ace Dry Cleaners, is still not sure if she
_____ her job. "I'm _____ right now," Mrs. Carson said.
　　2. quit　　　　　　　　　　3. decide -neg.
　　How _____ the Carsons _____ the money? First they _____ a long
　　　　　　　　　　　　　　4. spend　　　　　　　　　　　　5. take
vacation. They said they _____ because they like their neighborhood. However, they _____
　　　　　　　　　　　6. move -neg.　　　　　　　　　　　　　　　　　　　　　　7. buy
two new cars. They're also _____ some money to their favorite charity.
　　　　　　　　　　　8. give
　　Mr. Carson said he thinks that the money _____ their lives easier. "We _____
　　　　　　　　　　　　　　　　　　　　　9. make　　　　　　　　　　10. worry -neg.
about money anymore." However, he knows that the money _____ some problems too. "A
　　　　　　　　　　　　　　　　　　　　　　　　　　11. cause
lot of people _____ us for money. What _____ we _____?"
　　　　　12. ask　　　　　　　　　　13. say

2   Read the article again. Ask and answer questions about the Carsons' plans:

A: Are the Carsons going to *take a vacation?*
B: *Yes,* they *are.*

3 Mrs. Carson is talking to Dave about their trip. Listen to their conversation and complete the itinerary.

Itinerary

Gregory and Martha Carson

DATE	DEPART	ARRIVE	AIRLINE	FLIGHT
May 15	Chicago	*Mexico City* 1	Eastern	___ 2
May ___ 3	Mexico City	Bogotá	Avianca	___ 4
May 29	___ 5	Rio de Janeiro	Brazilian Airlines	481
June 6	Rio de Janeiro	Madrid	Iberia	727
June 15	Madrid	London	British Airways	543
June 25	London	Cairo	Egypt Airlines	421

4 Look at the Carsons' itinerary for the first part of their trip. Ask and answer questions about their trip.

1. Where / go first
A: Where are they going to go first?
B: To Mexico City.

2. What airline / take
3. How long / stay in Mexico
4. When / leave Mexico
5. Where / go next
6. When / be in Madrid

5 Pretend you are a newspaper reporter. Interview a student who just won the lottery. Begin like this:

REPORTER: How much money did you win?
WINNER: *$5 million.*
REPORTER: How are you going to spend it?
WINNER: First, I'm going to *bring my family to this country.*
REPORTER: Are you going to *buy a house?*
WINNER: *Yes, I think so.*
REPORTER: . . .

B.

The Carsons	**might (not)** **may (not)**	go to Thailand. They aren't sure because Mr. Carson wants to go, but Mrs. Carson doesn't.

1 **The Carsons aren't sure what they want to do with their money. Talk about their ideas. Complete the sentences with *might, may, might not* or *may not*.**

1. They _may_ buy a big house. Mrs. Carson likes to have a lot of visitors.
2. They _____ buy a big car. Mr. Carson thinks big cars are safe and fun to drive.
3. Mrs. Carson _____ quit her job. She likes to work.
4. The Carsons _____ buy new furniture. Their furniture is very old.
5. The Carsons _____ travel every year. They enjoy their home and friends.

2 **Dave's parents are going to give him a surprise. Guess what it might be.**

A: What do you think the surprise is?
B: I'm not sure. It might be *a new car.*

3 **Look at the pictures and then talk to a classmate about weekend plans. Ask and answer questions like this:**

A: What are you going to do *on Saturday?*
B: I'm not sure. *Sam and I* might *go to the movies.*

4 **Dictation**

Dave's neighbor Tom always asks him personal questions. Listen to their conversation. Then listen again and write the questions Tom asks.

1. _____ ?
2. _____ ?
3. _____ ?
4. _____ ?

C.

The Carsons are happy.
  Steve and Julie are **too**.
	The Carsons aren't depressed.
	  Steve and Julie are**n't either**.

The Carsons might buy a house.
  Steve might **too**.
	Mrs. Carson might not buy a new car.
	  Steve might **not either**.

Dave likes jazz.
  Maria does **too**.
	Dave doesn't like disco music.
	  Maria does**n't either**.

Maria worked hard last weekend.
  Dave did **too**.
	Maria didn't watch much TV.
	  Dave did**n't either**.

1 a. How much do you remember about Dave and Maria? Write *yes* or *no* under each name.

	DAVE	MARIA
1. living in New York now?	*yes*	*yes*
2. born in New York?		
3. born in the United States?		
4. like(s) rock music?		
5. happy with present job?		
6. working?		
7. can speak Polish?		
8. saw Tina Turner's concert?		
9. won the lottery?		

b. Make sentences with *too* about items 1, 4 and 6:
1. *Dave's living in New York now. Maria is too.*

c. Make sentences with *not either* about items 2, 5 and 9:
2. *Dave wasn't born in New York. Maria wasn't either.*

d. Make sentences with *but* about items 3, 7 and 8:
3. *Dave was born in the United States, but Maria wasn't.*

2 Now look at the questions in Exercise 1a and answer them about yourself. Then compare your answers with a classmate's answers and make statements with *too*, *either* and *but*.

PUT IT ALL TOGETHER
Listen to the two parts of the conversation. Then listen to each part of it again. Say if the statements are right or wrong.

A. 1. Dave told Maria his news first.
  2. He was surprised at his parents' news.
  3. Dave's parents may take a trip around the world.
  4. They gave him a surprise present.

B. 1. Maria went to Igor Kessler's office.
  2. Maria is the only person that he is going to interview.
  3. She is going to begin working for Igor Kessler in two weeks.

ON YOUR OWN
Discuss these questions with your classmates.

1 Did you ever buy a lottery ticket? Did you ever win?

2 What are some advantages and disadvantages of lotteries?

3 Is there a lottery in your city or country? If so, who runs the lottery?

Reading

The Lucky Twenty-one

NEW YORK, Aug. 22—A special group of men just won part of New York's $41 million lottery. The men laughed and hugged each other when they showed lottery officials their winning
(5) ticket today.

These twenty-one winners are a special group because they all come from other countries. Celso Manuel Garcete, who chose the winning number, is from Paraguay. Peter Lee, who bought the
(10) tickets, is from Hong Kong. Others come from China, Czechoslovakia, Poland, Italy and Germany. They all work together at Hantscho Inc., a factory near New York City. And yesterday they decided to buy lottery tickets
(15) together.

Every man chose six numbers. Then each one gave Peter Lee his numbers and one dollar to buy a ticket. After Mr. Lee bought the tickets, all the members signed a contract. In the contract,
(20) they all agreed to share the prize money equally.

Each one in the winning group is going to receive $25,000 a year for the next twenty years. Some families plan to make a few changes with the money. "Maybe we'll bring my grandparents
(25) here now," said Anna Siwy, daughter of worker John Siwy. Mrs. Garcete might spend a few months with her family in Paraguay.

But most of the winners are going to continue their usual lives. John Pelczar is going to send
(30) his daughters to college. Pantaleo DeBiase plans to keep working. "It's not much money for a family of five," he told a reporter. And Willie Lao will just wait and see. "I'm too tired to decide right now," he said with a happy grin.

1 Comprehension. Answer these questions.

1. Why were the men so happy?
2. Where do the winners work?
3. What was in their contract?
4. How much money will each man receive?

2 Vocabulary building. Choose the word or phrase that means the same as the one underlined.

1. *(line 19)* All the members signed a contract.
   a. a letter
   b. a ticket
   c. an agreement

2. *(line 26)* Mrs. Garcete might spend a few months with her family in Paraguay.
   a. go shopping with
   b. visit
   c. buy things for

3. *(line 33)* Willie Lao will just wait and see.
   a. see his family
   b. decide later
   c. wait for a bus

4. *(line 34)* "I'm too tired to decide right now," he said with a happy grin.
   a. laugh
   b. face
   c. smile

3 Putting events in order. Number these events in the order they happened in the article.

1. _____ Mr. Lee paid for the tickets.
2. _____ A reporter interviewed the winners.
3. _1_ The workers decided to buy lottery tickets together.
4. _____ Each man chose six numbers, then gave Peter Lee one dollar to pay for the tickets.
5. _____ They showed the lottery officials their winning ticket.

4 Making inferences. Read the story again. Then try to guess the answers to these questions.

1. Are the winners close to their families?
2. Were the winners rich before they won the lottery?
3. Did they get very rich after they won the lottery?

Writing

Skill: Grouping ideas into paragraphs
Task: Writing a letter confirming plans

When you write, it's important to divide your
information into paragraphs. Each paragraph should
tell about one idea.

1 Read the letter.

> Dear Jennie,
>
>   I'm so glad you're coming to Toronto next week. Here are some
> things we can do.
>   On the first day, we can visit the CN Tower in the morning. During
> lunch, we can talk about our afternoon plans. After we eat, we can go to
> the Royal Ontario Museum, or we can tour the Ontario Science Center. In
> the evening, we're going to go to Roy Thomson Hall for a concert.
>   The second day you might be tired, so we can stay home and relax in
> the morning. In the afternoon, we can tour the city by bus.
>   You don't have much time, so we can see only a few sights. But it's
> going to be fun!
>
>   See you soon,
>
>   Sylvia

**Paragraph One is an introduction. Paragraph Four is a conclusion. What do
Paragraphs Two and Three talk about?**

2 **With a classmate, make some plans for an outing in a city you both know
    well. Make two lists—one for morning activities, one for afternoon activities.
    Here are some suggestions:**

1. Eat lunch in an outdoor café or in a
   restaurant at the top of a skyscraper.
2. Go window shopping at an expensive store.

3. Visit a park.
4. Tour a famous old building.

3 **Now write a letter to your classmate about your plans for the outing. Your
    letter will have four paragraphs:**

| Paragraph One | Introduction | Paragraph Three | Afternoon plans |
| Paragraph Two | Morning plans | Paragraph Four | Conclusion |

**Follow the model in Exercise 1. Remember the words you already practiced—
and, but, so, first, next, when, during and *after*.**

For pronunciation exercises for Unit 7, see page 112.

1 Steve is visiting Dave. Listen to their conversation.

1

DAVE: Did you get your check from Mom and Dad yet?

STEVE: No, not yet. Dad said it might be here today.

DAVE: What are you and Julie going to do with the money?

STEVE: Well, first we're going to move to a bigger place. We'd like to buy a house, but it's a lot more expensive than an apartment.

DAVE: Mom and Dad said they have a surprise for me.

STEVE: Do you know what it is?

DAVE: No. Oh, there's the doorbell.

2

DAVE: Dad! What are you doing here?

MR. CARSON: I had to make a delivery.

DAVE: A delivery? Where's Mom?

MR. CARSON: She's over there by your new truck.

DAVE: You mean that truck is *mine?*

MR. CARSON: Of course it's yours.

3

DAVE: It's incredible! I can't think of a better gift. Thanks.

MR. CARSON: We're glad you like it. And here's your check, Steve.

STEVE: Thanks, Dad! I'm going to put it in our savings account right away.

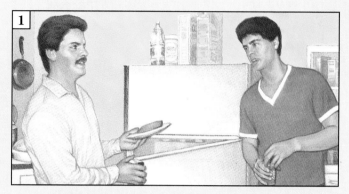

2 Say *That's right, That's wrong* or *It doesn't say*.

1. Steve and Julie think apartments are nicer than houses.
2. Steve and Julie live in a nice neighborhood.
3. Dave was surprised when he saw his father.
4. Dave didn't like his gift.

3 Warm Up

Thank someone for a gift.

A: Oh, *a TV!* What *a great* gift! Thanks a lot!

B: I'm glad you like *it*.   OR   You're welcome.

DEVELOP YOUR VOCABULARY

generous	wonderful
terrific	perfect
thoughtful	. . .

Practice

A.

clean → cleaner nice → nicer big → bigger pretty → prettier	Steve and Julie want a **cleaner** neighborhood. They want to live in a **nicer** place. They want a **bigger** apartment. They want a **prettier** apartment.
more expensive **more** careful	Steve and Julie are getting a **more expensive** place. Julie is a careful driver, but Maria is **more careful.**
good → **better** bad → **worse**	Dave needed a **better** truck. Roberto is a bad driver, but Dave is **worse.**

1 Steve has more money now. What can he do? Look at the pictures and make sentences with the comparative of the adjectives in the box and the verbs below each picture.

beautiful	large
expensive	nice
good	

1. Steve can *rent a larger apartment.*

1. rent

2. live

3. buy

4. shop

5. eat

2 Write four to six sentences about how you would like to change your life. Use the comparative of the adjectives in the box. Then tell a classmate.

I'd like to *live in a bigger city.*

beautiful	clean	expensive	long	pretty
big	easy	good	nice	safe

B.

The Austin is	**more practical**	**than**	the Supersport.
The Supersport is	**smaller**		the Austin.

1   Steve and Julie are going to buy a new car. Steve wants to buy the Supersport, and Julie wants to buy the Austin. Listen to their conversation and say which car is better in each category.

	SUPERSPORT	AUSTIN
efficient		✓
cheap		
exciting		
practical		
reliable		
fast		
big		

2   Now compare the two cars like this. Remember to use *than*.

The *Austin* is *more efficient* than the *Supersport*.

3   Now look at the information about these two refrigerators. Decide which one you would like to buy. Discuss your decision with a classmate.

Name	Price	Size	Freezer size	Efficiency rating
Polar	$904	20 cu. ft.	4 cu. ft.	good
Arctic	$750	18 cu. ft.	3½ cu. ft.	fair

freezer

refrigerator

A: I think the Polar is *better* than the Arctic.
B: But the Arctic is *cheaper* than the Polar.

C.

Mr. and Mrs. Carson gave	the check **to Steve.** it **to him.** **Steve** the check. **him** the check.
Mr. and Mrs. Carson bought	a truck **for Dave.** it **for him.** **Dave** a truck. **him** a truck.

Other verbs that can take _to_:		
bring	sell	take
owe	send	teach
pay	show	

Other verbs that can take _for_:		
bake	find	draw
build	get	make

Note: You cannot say, _They gave him it._

1 Look at the pictures and say what these people did.

1. Barbara gave a tripod to Dave.
   OR   Barbara gave Dave a tripod.

1. Barbara / give tripod / Dave

2. Maria / show her dress designs / Igor Kessler

3. Dave / give a ride / Maria

4. Yolanda / buy a football / Ricky

5. Julie / make a table / Mr. Carson

6. Steve / teach math / his daughter

2 Look again at the pictures in Exercise 1. Then ask and answer questions with the words below.

1. Barbara / camera bag / Dave

A: Did Barbara give Dave a camera bag?
B: No, she gave him a tripod.

2. Maria / shirts / Igor Kessler

3. Dave / ring / Maria
4. Yolanda / bicycle / Ricky
5. Julie / chair / Mr. Carson
6. Steve / Spanish / his daughter

3 Ask a classmate about a present he or she gave someone.

A: What did you give your _daughter for her birthday?_
B: I _got her a bicycle._

DEVELOP YOUR VOCABULARY

baked _him_ a pie
built _them_ a bookcase
drew _them_ a picture
sent _her_ a magazine subscription
. . .

Just for Fun

**4 Sentence scramble. How fast can you unscramble each set
of words to make one *true* sentence?**

1. her designs   Maria   showed   Igor Kessler
2. Dave   to   gave   the Carsons   their itinerary
3. gave   Ricky   a bath   his dog
4. a customer   a necklace   Yolanda   sold

D.

	my		mine.
	your		yours.
This is	his	present. It's	his.
	her		hers.
	their		theirs.
	our		ours.

**1 Mr. and Mrs. Carson bought some
presents. They are putting names on
them. Complete their conversation with
mine, yours, his, hers or *theirs*.**

MR. CARSON: Is this Dave's present?

MRS. CARSON: No, it's Julie's.

MR. CARSON: How do you know?

MRS. CARSON: Because *hers* is the one with the red ribbon. Dave's has a blue
                     ——
                     1
                     ribbon.

MR. CARSON: Is this Steve's?

MRS. CARSON: No. _____ is in the blue box. That's Sara and Bill's. I remember
                         2
                     because _____ doesn't have a ribbon.
                             3

MR. CARSON: What about this one?

MRS. CARSON: Oh, that's a special one. It's _____ .
                                        4

MR. CARSON: _____ ! Why did you buy *me* a present?
               5

MRS. CARSON: Because you're such a wonderful husband. That's why.

**2 Ask and answer questions like these about the presents. Use the information
in Exercise 1 and in the picture.**

A: Is the *white box with the blue ribbon Dave's?*   A: Is the *green box Lynn's?*
B: Yes, it's *his.*   B: No. *Hers* is the *pink box with the white ribbon.*

3 Ask to borrow something, and your classmate will make an excuse.

A: I forgot my *English book.* Can I borrow yours?
B: I'm sorry. *Mine is at home too.* Why don't you ask *Tom?*
A: I did. *He lost his.*

Student B can use these excuses:

Mine is broken.
Mine doesn't work.
Dave has mine.
I'm using mine.

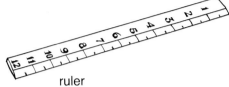
ruler

pencil sharpener

eraser

scissors

calculator

4 Review and Build

Steve and Julie are moving to a new apartment. Listen to this commercial for a moving company and complete it.

Are you moving?

Do you need careful, ———— movers?
                        1
Then call Acme Moving Company.

We're ———— ———— than the others, and we're ———— too. ———— ———— are we?
         2   3   4   5   6
Call ———— for a free estimate. Make our moving company ———— .
       7   8
That's Acme Moving Company. We're ———— ———— with your furniture ———— you are.
                                     9   10   11

Just for Fun

5 Write a commercial for a product or service. Then perform it for your class.

Some services

car repair	delivery service
taxi	beauty shop
airline	

Some products

cars	beverages
refrigerators	soap
clothes	

Life Skills

Banking

For Your Information

Checking accounts and money orders

If you want to open a *checking account,* you *deposit* (put) money into the bank and then the bank gives you checks. You can use the checks to *withdraw* (take) money from the bank and to pay bills.

If you do not have a checking account, you can pay your bills with *money orders.* You can buy a money order at a bank or post office and use it in place of cash.

1 Judy Chen doesn't have a checking account. She's buying a money order to pay her rent to J. R. Apartments Inc. Listen to Judy and the bank teller and complete their conversation.

JUDY: I'd like __to__ __buy__ a money order.
                1   2

TELLER: For how much?

JUDY: _____ .
           3

TELLER: OK. There's a _____ service charge.
                    4

JUDY: Here's _____ .
              5

TELLER: And here's your _____ _____ . Just
                       6   7
        fill it out.

JUDY: _____ _____ .
         8   9

THE LENOX SAVINGS BANK
NEW YORK, NEW YORK   No. BX 272516
THIS MONEY ORDER MUST BE PRESENTED WITHIN 90 DAYS
SAVINGS BANK MONEY ORDER
DATE   PAY $
NOT GOOD FOR AMOUNTS OVER FIVE HUNDRED DOLLARS ($500.)
PAY TO THE ORDER OF _____
REMITTER MUST INSERT PAYEE'S NAME ON ABOVE LINE
REMITTER'S SIGNATURE _____
⑆0000089⑆ 34539⑈   ADDRESS _____

Now roleplay the situation above.

2 Judy decided to open a checking account. A bank clerk is asking her questions. Listen to their conversation and complete the form.

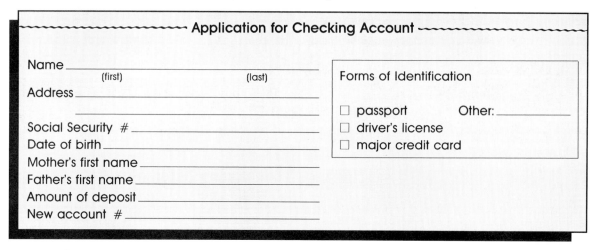

Now roleplay the situation above.
Student A wants to open an account.
Student B is the bank clerk. Use the application form to ask questions.

3 Steve has a checking account at Metropolis Bank. He wants to cash a check. Read his conversation with the teller.

STEVE: I'd like to cash this check for *$100.00*.
TELLER: Oh, you forgot to endorse it. Please sign the back.
STEVE: OK. Here you are.
TELLER: Fine. How would you like your money?
STEVE: *In tens*, please.

For Your Information
Getting change

At the bank, you can ask for your money in different ways. For example, if you want $100, you can say:

"In tens, please."

OR

"One fifty, two twenties and a ten."

You can also be less exact and ask for your money in "big" bills or "small" bills. If it is not important to you, you can say "It doesn't matter."

Now practice the conversation above with a classmate. Use the information in the pictures.

a. $120.00

b. $50.00

c. $200.00

d. $350.00

e. $30.00

ON YOUR OWN
Discuss these questions with your classmates.

1 How do you like to pay for things—by check? money order? cash? credit card? What are some advantages and disadvantages of each?

2 How do people usually pay for things in the country you are in now? In the country you come from?

For pronunciation exercises for Unit 8, see page 112.

REVIEW 4 _____

1 Dave is talking to Maria. Complete their conversation. Use *be going to* and the verbs.

DAVE: What _____are_____ you _____going to do_____ next Friday night?
                                        1. do

MARIA: I think I _____ home and work on some designs. Why?
                    2. stay

DAVE: Oh. I wanted to invite you to Steve and Julie's. They _____ a special dinner.
                                                              3. make

MARIA: Sounds like fun. _____ your parents _____ there too?
                                                      4. be

DAVE: Yes. They _____ for Chicago until Sunday.
                 5. leave -neg.

MARIA: That's good. How _____ we _____ there? By bus?
                                         6. get

DAVE: No. We _____ in my new truck!
             7. ride

MARIA: Your new truck! Congratulations! But, I hope you _____ carefully, Dave.
                                                          8. drive

DAVE: Don't worry. We _____ a safe ride and a good time.
                       9. have

2 Look at Julie Carson's list of things to do before they move. Then write sentences saying what Julie *is going to* do and what she *might* do.

She's going to make a new table.
She might invite the Drews for dinner.

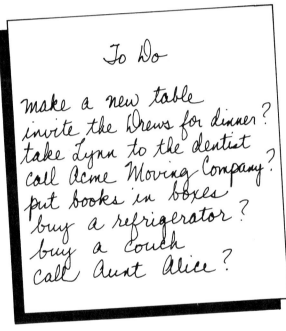

To Do

make a new table
invite the Drews for dinner?
take Lynn to the dentist
call Acme Moving Company?
put books in boxes
buy a refrigerator?
buy a couch
call Aunt Alice?

3 Look at the chart about Steve and Julie. Then match the information in columns A and B and write sentences. Add commas and periods when necessary.

	Steve	Julie
speak Spanish	✓	X
smoke	X	X
run in marathon	✓	✓
drive a car	✓	✓
cook	X	✓
study art	X	X

A
1. _d_ Steve speaks Spanish,
2. ___ Steve doesn't smoke
3. ___ Steve ran in a marathon
4. ___ Steve drives a car
5. ___ Steve can't cook
6. ___ Steve didn't study art

B
a. Julie did too.
b. Julie doesn't either.
c. Julie didn't either.
d. but Julie doesn't.
e. Julie does too.
f. but Julie can.

1. Steve speaks Spanish, but Julie doesn't.

Now compare yourself to Steve. Use *not either, too* or *but*.

4 Complete this conversation. Use the comparative form of the adjective. Add *than* when necessary.

MR. CARSON: Why don't you, Julie and the kids move to Chicago? It's _nicer than_
                New York.   1. nice

STEVE: But we think New York is _____ Chicago.
                                        2. interesting

MR. CARSON: But Chicago is _____ New York.
                            3. beautiful

STEVE: Maybe. But the winters in Chicago are _____.
                                                    4. cold

MR. CARSON: But life in Chicago is _____. It's _____ New York too.
                                    5. easy   6. clean

STEVE: New York is _____, and it's _____.
                        7. big   8. exciting

MR. CARSON: Sure. And it's _____ to do all those exciting things!
                            9. expensive

STEVE: Sorry, Dad. I still think New York is _____ Chicago.
                                                    10. good

5 Complete these sentences with *for* or *to*. Then rewrite them in a different way.

1. Yolanda sold a necklace _to_ a customer.

Yolanda sold a customer a necklace.

2. Barbara sent a letter _____ a friend.
3. The Carsons gave presents _____ their children.

4. Maria made a dress _____ Barbara.
5. Dave bought a book _____ Steve.
6. Julie baked a cake _____ her family.

6 Change the words in italics to a possessive pronoun.

1. This is *Dave's truck*.   _his_
2. These are *Maria's T-shirts*.   _____
3. Is this *your book?*   _____
4. Are these *the Carsons' tickets?*   _____
5. This is *my pen*.   _____
6. This is *yours and mine*.   _____

Just for Fun

7 How many comparisons can you make for each of these pairs of words? Use your imagination and your dictionary, if necessary.

1. lemon / orange

A lemon is smaller than an orange.
An orange is sweeter than a lemon.
An orange is more expensive than a lemon.
A lemon is . . .

2. dog / cat
3. rain / snow
4. pencil / cigarette
5. night / day
6. spaghetti / grass
7. diamonds / glass

9 A Lucky Break

1 Roberto just came home from work. He is talking to Yolanda. Listen to their conversation.

1

ROBERTO: I called you tonight about 10:00, but there was no answer.

YOLANDA: At 10:00? Oh, I was taking a shower. Why did you call?

ROBERTO: A man from Vivitar Records was in the club while we were playing.

YOLANDA: Really?

ROBERTO: Yes. And . . . he thinks we're very good! He thinks maybe we can make a record for them.

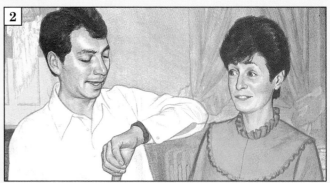

2

YOLANDA: Oh, Roberto! That's great. What a lucky break! Let's call your mother.

ROBERTO: We can't call now. It's too late.

YOLANDA: She doesn't go to bed this early. I'm sure she's watching TV.

ROBERTO: Yeah. You're probably right.

3

MOTHER: Hello?

ROBERTO: Hi, Mom. I'm sorry. I know it's late.

MOTHER: That's OK. I was just watching TV. What's the matter?

ROBERTO: Vivitar Records may offer us a contract.

MOTHER: Oh, that's wonderful!

ROBERTO: Well, it's not definite yet. We have to audition this Wednesday.

2 Say *That's right*, *That's wrong* or *It doesn't say.*

1. Yolanda wasn't home when Roberto called.
2. The man from Vivitar liked Roberto's band.
3. Roberto's mother usually goes to bed late.
4. Vivitar Records is going to give Roberto's band a contract.

3 Warm Up

Apologize and give an excuse.

A: I'm sorry, *Ms. Bonner. I didn't do my homework.* I was too *tired.*

B: I understand. *You can bring it tomorrow.*

DEVELOP YOUR VOCABULARY

exhausted	ill
upset	busy
preoccupied	. . .

Practice

A.

It's **very** late, but I think I can call.
It's **too** late. I can't call now.

1 Say what each person can't do and why.

1. Dave can't go to work. He's too sick.

1. go to work

2. go to the movies

3. vote

4. cut the grass

5. reach the shelf

6. dive into the pool

2 Yolanda was very excited about Roberto's news, so she called her friend Judy. Complete their conversation with *too* or *very*. Use *too* where you can.

YOLANDA: I have some _____ *very* _____ exciting news. I wanted to call you last night, but it was
          1

          _____ late. Roberto's band is going to make a record!
          2

JUDY: That's great! I knew it. Your husband is going to be a _____ famous
                                                                    3

          musician some day.

YOLANDA: Not _____ famous, I hope. Successful musicians have to travel a lot.
              4

JUDY: Well, don't worry about that now. How does Roberto feel? I'm sure he's

          _____ happy.
          5

YOLANDA: Happy? He couldn't sleep last night. He was _____ excited.
                                                        6

**3 Yolanda is helping Roberto buy a new sweater to wear at the audition.
Listen to their conversation and say which one they decide to buy.**

1

2

3

Just for Fun

4 Say which painting you like. See if your classmate agrees.

A: I like *Drowning Girl.* What about you?
B: No, it's *too modern* for me.
   OR   Yes, it's very . . .

DEVELOP YOUR VOCABULARY

abstract	violent
old-fashioned	original
dramatic	. . .
colorful	

Roy Lichtenstein. 1963
1. *Drowning Girl*

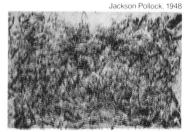
Jackson Pollock. 1948
2. *Number 1, 1948*

© Prado Museum-Madrid
3. *Guernica*

4. *The Musicians*

5. *Scholar by a Waterfall*

B.

What	**were** you **was** he	**doing** at 2:00 yesterday?	I He	**was working.**
Were they **watching** TV?			Yes, they **were.** No, they **weren't.**	

1 Maria was busy yesterday. Look at the list of her activities. Then listen to the conversations and match each activity with the correct time.

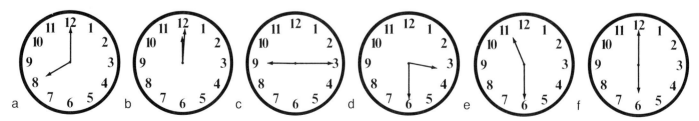

a   b   c   d   e   f

1. _____ watch TV
2. _____ wait for the bus
3. _____ talk to Dave on the telephone
4. _*a*_ clean the house
5. _____ prepare dinner
6. _____ have lunch with Yolanda

2 **Now look at the information in Exercise 1 and ask and answer questions about Maria.**

1. A: What was Maria doing at *8:00?*
   B: She was *cleaning the house.*

3 **Pretend a friend called you, but there was no answer. Say what you were doing.**

FRIEND: I called you *at 3:00,* but there was no answer. *Were you sleeping?*
YOU: Yes, I was.
OR No. I was *shopping, and my husband was taking a nap.*

C.

| What **was** Mrs. Ruiz **doing when** Roberto **called?** | She **was watching** TV **when** he **called.** |

| He called **while** she **was watching** TV. |

1 **Interview these people and ask them what they were doing when something important happened.**

1. YOU: Maria, what were you doing when the designer called?
   MARIA: I was washing my hair (when he called).

1. Maria / designer called

4. Yolanda / you met Roberto

2. Mr. Carson / you found out about the lottery

5. Dave / Roberto called to ask you to be in his band

3. Dave / your father called with the good news

2 **Now ask and answer questions about the people in Exercise 1.**

1. A: When did the designer call Maria?
   B: He called while she was washing her hair.

3 Ask a friend about what he or she was doing when they met someone for the first time.

A: What were you doing when you met *Juan?*
B: I was *standing outside the classroom.*

PUT IT ALL TOGETHER
Yolanda is calling Roberto's mother to give her some important news. Listen to their conversation and complete the newspaper article.

East Harlem News / A community newspaper

♪ Music Notes
by Harold Carter

LOCAL GROUP SIGNS RECORD CONTRACT

Local band, Los Santos, signed a record contract with Vivitar Records yesterday. Bandleader Roberto Ruiz said that the men in the band know they are ___very___ lucky. He explained that an agent from
1
Vivitar _____ in the audience one night _____ they _____
2   3   4
_____ . "He _____ _____ in front, and I could see he
5   6   7
_____ _____ the music. Then after we _____ , he came
8   9   10
to talk to us. It was really a lucky break."

You can hear Los Santos at the Purple Note. Go see them now

before it's _____ late.
11

ON YOUR OWN
Discuss these questions with your classmates.

1 Name two successful people. Why do you think they are successful?

2 What does success mean to you? Are there kinds of success other than financial success? What would you like to be successful at?

Reading

U-p-b-e-a-t

From Street Fair to Studio: Local Group Makes Good

by Anita Brilla

Upbeat's Top Ten of the Week

1. "Are You Sure?"
   —Harmony
2. "I Want to Go Dancing"
   —the Orlons
3. "Out of Place"—Mary Monk
4. "I'm Not Either"
   —the Valentines
5. "Good Money"—Orlando X
6. "Wait and See"—the Gee Bees
7. "We Haven't Got Much Time"
   —Stevie Wander
8. "That's Right"
   —Maggie Jackson
9. "Change of Heart"
   —Los Santos
10. "Don't Worry about That"
    —Sisters

The ninth place in our Top Ten this week is "Change of Heart" by Los Santos. A neighborhood group, Los Santos have moved (5) fast—from a local street fair to a professional recording studio in only one year.

The musicians are all members of our East Harlem community. (10) They met about a year ago when guitarist Johnny Castillo was performing at a street fair on East 125 Street. The group's singer, Luis Madeira, was selling hot dogs (15) nearby and asked to perform with him. The two hit it off right away, and a crowd started to gather. Castillo and Madeira performed all afternoon. Roberto Ruiz, another (20) neighborhood musician, was in that crowd. After the two finished, he invited them to practice with him. "We worked well together from the start," says Ruiz.

(25) The three were soon performing in local clubs like the Black Jacket Club and the Purple Note. Last winter drummer Dave Carson joined the group, and it was his (30) beat that made Vivitar Records notice the group.

"Change of Heart" has a mixed style. The music and words are romantic, but the beat is strong. (35) It's a great combination—colorful but not too wild—and it made me want to start dancing.

This new single is a good start for Los Santos. Vivitar is (40) promising an album in the fall. Look for it.

1 Comprehension. Complete the sentences.

1. Los Santos have become successful
   a. quickly.
   b. slowly.

2. The group members are all
   a. brothers.
   b. neighbors.

3. They met at a
   a. friend's house.
   b. street fair.

4. Los Santos' music
   a. combines different styles.
   b. is very wild.

5. In the fall, Los Santos are making
   a. a new single.
   b. an album.

2 Vocabulary building. Choose the word or phrase that means the same as the one underlined.

1. *(headline)* Local Group <u>Makes Good</u>
   a. is successful
   b. helps people

2. *(line 2)* She liked him at first, but then <u>she had a change of heart.</u>
   a. she liked him better
   b. she didn't like him anymore

3. *(line 16)* The two <u>hit it off</u> right away.
   a. started fighting
   b. became friends

4. *(line 17)* A crowd started to <u>gather.</u>
   a. come together
   b. leave

3 Finding the main idea and supporting details in a paragraph. Answer the questions.

Paragraph 1
1. Which sentence states the main idea?
   a. Los Santos succeeded very quickly.
   b. Los Santos played in a local street fair.

2. Which details support the main idea?
   a. The name of Los Santos's new record is "Change of Heart."
   b. Los Santos met last year and made a record this year.

Paragraph 4
1. The writer
   a. describes the musical style of "Change of Heart."
   b. tells what she doesn't like about "Change of Heart."

Paragraph 2
1. Which sentence contains the main idea?
   a. The first sentence.
   b. The last sentence.

2. How does the writer support her main idea?
   a. She tells a story about how the group members met.
   b. She tells us the musicians' names.

2. For each detail, say *yes* or *no*. "Change of Heart"
   a. has romantic music and words.
   b. is not good for dancing.
   c. has a strong beat.

Just for Fun

4 The song titles in "Upbeat's Top Ten" are all expressions from units in this book. Here are the units they are from:

1. "Are You Sure?" page 2
2. "I Want to Go Dancing," page 27
3. "Out of Place," page 38
4. "I'm Not Either," page 60
5. "Good Money," page 8
6. "Wait and See," page 61
7. "We Haven't Got Much Time," page 46
8. "That's Right," page 2
9. "Change of Heart," page 79
10. "Don't Worry about That," page 50

Do you remember what they mean? Choose three titles. Then work with a classmate and write a conversation that shows what each title means.

1. *Are you sure?*

A: I don't want to go to the movies tonight.
B: Are you sure?
A: Yes. I'm really tired.

Writing

Skill: Supporting an opinion
Task: Writing a letter of complaint

When you write a letter of complaint, you express your opinion.

1   Read the letter.

> 321 E. 18th Street
> New York, NY 10003
> June 29, 1988
>
> Customer Service Department
> National Bank
> 64 West 4th Street
> New York, NY 10003
>
> Dear Sir or Madam:
>   I am a customer of National Bank, and I am writing to complain about your service. In my opinion, National Bank's service is very slow and inconvenient.
>   Yesterday I went to your bank to cash my paycheck. While I was waiting in line, two of the tellers left for lunch. I stood in line for twenty minutes, but when it was finally my turn, the teller told me he could not help me. He was going to lunch too. Then the next teller told me the bank did not cash paychecks that day, and I had to wait until today.
>   Because of my experience at National, I am planning to change to another bank.
>
>   Very truly yours,
>
>   Cheung Han

2   Discuss these questions with a classmate.

1. What is the writer's opinion of National Bank's service?
2. How does the writer explain and support his opinion?
3. Does he write his opinion at the beginning or the end of the letter?
4. What connecting words does the writer use in his explanation?

3   Who or what do you want to complain about? Your local bus service? Dog owners in your neighborhood? Your telephone service? Write a letter of complaint—give your opinion and support that opinion with a story about your own experience.

Paragraph One	Introduction — What is your complaint?
Paragraph Two	Your experience — What were you doing? (Use *while—While I was waiting for a bus . . . While I was walking to work . . .*) — What happened while you were doing that? — Then what happened? (Make sure your story has at least two steps.)
Paragraph Three	Conclusion — What are you going to do about your complaint? — What do you want them to do?

For pronunciation exercises for Unit 9, see page 112.

1 Maria, Yolanda and Dave are having coffee. Listen to their conversation.

1

DAVE: Have you seen any good movies lately?

YOLANDA: I saw *Blue Sunrise* last weekend. I thought it was great. Have you seen it?

DAVE: No, I haven't, but I'd like to. They say it's really exciting. Have you seen it, Maria?

MARIA: Pardon? Oh, I'm sorry. I wasn't listening.

2

DAVE: You seem quiet today. Are you OK?

MARIA: Not really. I've got an upset stomach, and I feel really tired.

YOLANDA: Do you have a fever?

MARIA: Well, I feel a little warm and achy.

DAVE: You look a little pale too.

3

YOLANDA: It sounds like you're getting the flu. Have you taken any medicine?

MARIA: No, I haven't. When I take aspirin, it upsets my stomach.

YOLANDA: Then you should take this. It doesn't have any aspirin in it. Here.

DAVE: And you should go home and rest. I can drive you home.

MARIA: I think that's a good idea.

2 Answer the questions.

1. Who saw *Blue Sunrise?*
2. Did she like it?
3. Why's Maria quiet?
4. Why can't she take aspirin?
5. What's she going to do now?

3 Give a sick friend advice.

A: You look *awful.*

B: I know. *I have a sore throat.*

A: Why don't you *call the doctor?*

DEVELOP YOUR VOCABULARY

I have a	stomachache	fever
	toothache	cough
	cold	. . .
I feel	dizzy	faint
	nauseous	. . .

Practice

A.

I You They	have(n't)	
He She	has(n't)	**seen** *Blue Sunrise*.

Have you (ever) **seen** *Rocky?*	Yes, I **have**. No, I **haven't**.
When **did** you **see** it?	I **saw** it **last year**.

I have = I've	I have not = I haven't
you have = you've	he has not = he hasn't
they have = they've	
she has = she's	

1 Dave and Maria are at Maria's apartment now. Dave wants to watch a
videotape. He's asking Maria what she has seen. Listen to their conversation.
Then check the movies Maria has and hasn't seen.

	has seen	hasn't seen
E.T.	✓	
Rocky		
Annie Hall		
The Godfather		
Superman		

2 Now make statements like this:

Maria has seen *E.T.* She hasn't . . .

3 Invite a classmate to a movie you want to see.

A: Why don't we go to a movie? Have you seen
Rambo?

B: No, I haven't. That's a good idea.
   OR   No, I haven't, but it's *too violent*.
   OR   Yes, I have. I saw it *last weekend.*

4 Match the base form of the verb with its past participle.

Base form	Past participle
1. _c_ see	a. written
2. ___ speak	b. been
3. ___ have	c. seen
4. ___ study	d. talked
5. ___ make	e. done
6. ___ be	f. eaten
7. ___ talk	g. read
8. ___ do	h. had
9. ___ eat	i. made
10. ___ go	j. spoken
11. ___ write	k. studied
12. ___ read	l. gone

Just for Fun

5 Ask your classmates questions about things they have done:

1. A: Have you ever *been to the Statue of Liberty?*
   B: Yes, I have.   OR   No, I haven't.

Find someone who has:

1. been to the Statue of Liberty

2. climbed a mountain

3. ridden a motorcycle

4. seen a shooting star

5. gone ice skating

6. used chopsticks

B.

Maria	doesn't **feel well.** doesn't **look well.** **seems unhappy.**

This medicine	**tastes bad.** **smells terrible.**

> **Note:** *Well* after *feel, look, sound* and *seem* is an adjective meaning *healthy.*

1 Look at the pictures and make statements about them.

1. Maria feels tired.

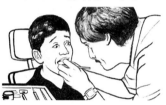

1. Maria / feel

2. Ricky / look

3. hamburger / taste

4. Maria / seem

5. soup / smell

6. music / sound

2 Read the conversation between Maria and her mother. Complete it with the correct verb and an appropriate adjective from the box. You can use an adjective more than once.

well   good   terrible   awful   delicious

MOTHER: How are you doing, Maria?

MARIA: I don't ___*feel*___ very ___*well*___, Mom.
              1. feel / sound   2

MOTHER: No, you don't _____ very _____. You're pale. And you
                      3. look / sound   4

        _____ _____. You should take some cough medicine.
        5. look / sound   6

MARIA: I know. Can you get me some?

MOTHER: OK. And you should eat something too. Do you want some tea or toast?

MARIA: No, nothing _____ _____.
                   7. feel / sound   8

(A few minutes later, Maria's mother comes back with orange juice and cough medicine.)

MOTHER: How about this juice?

MARIA: Oh, that _____ _____, Mom. It _____ _____ too.
            9. sound / look   10   11. sound / taste   12
        Thanks a lot.

3 Look at the pictures and answer the questions like this:

Who . . .

1. has worked all night?

I think it's Maria. She looks tired.

2. just got good news?
3. needs to see a doctor?
4. is going to take a big test?
5. just got some bad news?
6. just had a big argument?

C.

Maria has a fever. What **should** she do?	She	**should** take aspirin. **shouldn't** go to work.

1 Ask for and give advice by using the words in column A and column B or your own words.

A: I have *a cold*. What should I do?

B: When you have *a cold*, you should *drink juice*. And you shouldn't *wash your hair*.

A	B
1. cold	a. go to the doctor
2. headache	b. drink juice
3. upset stomach	c. go outside
4. small burn	d. walk around
5. sore throat	e. take aspirin
6. cough	f. drink tea with honey
7. fever	g. wash your hair
8. sprained ankle	h. put ice on it
	i. put a Band-Aid on it
	j. go swimming
	k. go to work
	l. stay in bed

2   Your friend has a problem. Find out what it is and give him or her advice.

YOU: What's the matter?
FRIEND: I'm worried about *my son. He's not
          doing well in school.* What should I do?
YOU: Have you *talked to his teacher?*
FRIEND: No.   OR   FRIEND: Yes.
YOU: Maybe you should.   YOU: Maybe you should also *get him a tutor.*

Your friend can use these ideas:

I'm worried about:	
my schoolwork	my parents
my future	my health
money	my job

3   Review and Build

**Ricky is at the doctor's. Read the questions. Then listen to the conversation
and answer the questions.**

1. What can't Ricky do? Why?

He can't do his schoolwork. When he reads, he
gets a headache.

2. What might he need?
3. What should he do?
4. Why shouldn't he feel bad?
5. What can't he do with ordinary glasses?
6. What should Ricky do about his problem?

ordinary glasses

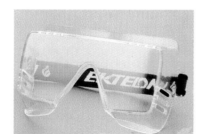
safety glasses

contact lenses

Life Skills

Health care

1 **Maria still feels sick. She called her doctor to make an appointment. Read the statements. Then listen to the conversation and say *That's right, That's wrong* or *It doesn't say.***

1. Maria spoke to the doctor.
2. Dr. Pérez is a man.
3. Dr. Pérez is very busy.
4. Maria is going to see Dr. Pérez next Monday.

For Your Information
Health clinics

Many people go to *health clinics* for medical care. Clinics are usually less expensive than private doctors. Clinics accept *health insurance* such as Medicaid and Medicare. For people who do not have insurance, there is often a *sliding scale*. This means that your *fee* (the money that you pay) depends on your *income* (the money that you make).

2 **Next Maria called a health clinic. Listen to the conversation and complete it.**

NURSE: West Side Clinic.

MARIA: Hello. I'd like to make an

**appointment** to see a doctor.
        1

NURSE: _____ you ever _____ here before?
        2   3

MARIA: No, I _____.
            4

NURSE: What seems to be the _____?
                            5

MARIA: Well, I've got a _____, and I feel very
                       6

_____ and achy. I also have a bad
  7

_____.
  8

NURSE: OK. You don't need an appointment.

Our hours are _____ to _____,
              9   10

Monday through _____. But you
                11

_____ come early. There are usually a
  12

lot of people.

MARIA: How much is the visit going to _____?
                                       13

NURSE: Do you have any health _____?
                                14

MARIA: No, I don't.

NURSE: Then it depends on your income. We

have a sliding scale from _____ to
                          15

_____.
  16

MARIA: Thank you.

Now roleplay a similar situation.

WEST SIDE CLINIC				
PATIENT'S NAME LAST		FIRST	DATE OF BIRTH	SEX
Gorska		Maria	5/14/68	F
PATIENT'S ADDRESS	APT. NO.	CITY	STATE	ZIP	TELEPHONE NO.
27 W. 76 St.	4-B	NY	NY	10023	877-6211
OCCUPATION	EMPLOYER'S NAME	EMPLOYER'S ADDRESS	TELEPHONE NO.
waitress/designer	V.I.P. Diner	2136 Broadway	787-3395
INCOME	NO. OF DEPENDENTS	HEALTH INSURANCE	SOCIAL SECURITY NO.
$10,000	0	none	542-79-6480
PERSON TO CONTACT IN EMERGENCY	RELATIONSHIP TO PATIENT	TELEPHONE NO.
Wanda Gorska	mother	877-6211

3 Maria is now at the clinic. Look at the form on page 88 and ask and answer questions like this with a classmate. Use your own information.

NURSE: What's your last name?
PATIENT: *Gorska.*

4 The doctor asked Maria about her medical history. Ask and answer questions like this:

DOCTOR: Have you ever had *the measles?*
PATIENT: Yes, I have. I had *the measles in 1978.*
    OR   No, I haven't.

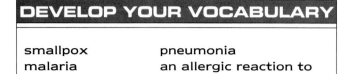

DEVELOP YOUR VOCABULARY

smallpox	pneumonia
malaria	an allergic reaction to
tuberculosis (TB)	any medicine

5 Look at the medicine labels. Then complete each statement.

1. Maria has to
   a. take 6 tablets a day.
   b. take 2 tablets a day.
   c. take 3 tablets a day.

2. The patient took one capsule at 8:00. She should take her next one at
   a. 8:30.
   b. 3:00.
   c. 11:00.

3. The patient should only
   a. take the medicine with a lot of bread.
   b. eat with a spoon.
   c. take the medicine when he eats or drinks milk.

4. The patient should probably not
   a. drive a car.
   b. take more than three capsules a day.
   c. take a capsule before bed.

5. The patient should not drink
   a. water.
   b. coffee.
   c. beer.

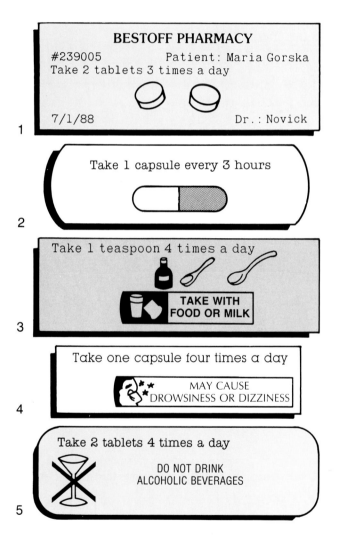

ON YOUR OWN
Discuss these questions with your classmates.

1 What do you do when you get sick? Do you go to a private doctor? A clinic? What are some advantages and disadvantages of each?

2 What qualities should a good doctor have? How can you find a good doctor?

For pronunciation exercises for Unit 10, see page 113.

REVIEW 5 _____

1 Answer these questions. Use *Yes* or *No* and *too* or *very*.

1. A: Did Yolanda buy a new coat?
   B: _No_. It was _too_ expensive.
2. A: Did Roberto's sweater cost a lot?
   B: _____. It was _____ expensive.
3. A: Did Ricky enjoy the movie?
   B: _____. It was _____ good.
4. A: Did Roberto and Yolanda go for a walk?
   B: _____. They were _____ tired.

5. A: Did Ricky go to bed early?
   B: _____. He was _____ tired.
6. A: Did Maria stay in bed all day?
   B: _____. She felt _____ sick.
7. A: Could the doctor see Maria?
   B: _____. The doctor was _____ busy.
8. A: Can Yolanda call Maria?
   B: _____. It's _____ late now.

2 Say what these people were doing yesterday.

1. 8:00 / Yolanda / newspaper

At 8:00, Yolanda was reading the newspaper.

2. 12:00 / Steve and Julie / lunch
3. 3:00 / Dave / the drums

4. 6:00 / Ricky / homework
5. 7:00 / Dave and Maria / TV
6. 8:00 / Roberto / coffee
7. 9:00 / I / . . .

3 Complete this conversation between Maria and her mother. Use the verbs and *when* or *while*.

MRS. GORSKA: What _were_ you _doing_ _when_ you met Dave for the
1. do   2. when / while
first time?

MARIA: I _____ T-shirts at the market.
3. sell

MRS. GORSKA: _____ Yolanda _____ there too?
4. work -neg.

MARIA: That's right. And Dave _____ her.
5. visit

MRS. GORSKA: But _____ Dave _____ in Yolanda's husband's band?
6. play -neg.

MARIA: Yes, but he _____ it full time. During the day he _____
7. do -neg.   8. work
for a construction company. _____ I met him, he _____
9. When / While   10. take
his lunch break. He came over to say hello to Yolanda _____
11. when / while
I _____ to her.
12. talk

4 Complete these charts with the correct forms of the verbs.

Present	Past Participle
see	seen
do	
have	
is	
	taken

Present	Past Participle
	gone
speak	
want	
	played

5 Look at Ricky Ruiz's medical chart. Then answer the questions.

1. A: Has Ricky ever had appendicitis?

   B: *Yes, he has. He had appendicitis in 1985.*

2. A: Has Ricky ever had the chicken pox?

   B: _____

3. A: Has Ricky ever had the measles?

   B: _____

Ricky Ruiz	
appendicitis	1985
the chicken pox	1983
the measles	—
the mumps	1984
tonsilitis	—

Now ask the questions.

4. A: _____

   B: Yes, he has. He had the mumps in 1984.

5. A: _____

   B: No, he hasn't.

6 Complete these sentences. Choose the correct verb and add an appropriate adjective.

1. Maria didn't *feel*   *well* , so she
   _{feel / smell}
   called the doctor.

2. That coffee _____ _____. Can I
   _{tastes / smells}
   have some?

3. I don't like that music. It _____
   _{seems / sounds}
   _____.

4. This milk _____ _____.
   _{sounds / tastes}
   Are you sure it's still good?

5. You _____ _____. Is that a new
   _{look / sound}
   sweater?

7 Match the problems in column A with the advice in column B. Complete the advice with *should* or *shouldn't*.

A

1. _b_ Dave has a headache.
2. ___ Ricky failed his last test.
3. ___ Roberto feels very nervous.
4. ___ Steve is very tired.
5. ___ Maria's brother wants to play in a band.

B

a. He _____ practice a lot.
b. He *should* take aspirin.
c. He _____ study more.
d. He _____ drink a lot of coffee.
e. He _____ go to bed late.

Just for Fun

8 Which word doesn't belong?

1. exhausted / depressed / (well) / tired
2. when / before / very / while
3. brother / designer / doctor / musician
4. eaten / gone / was / seen
5. smell / run / look / taste
6. cough / fever / stomachache / sick
7. should / want / could / might
8. haven't / shouldn't / wasn't / can

1 Maria and Yolanda are talking on the phone. Listen to their conversation.

1

YOLANDA:	Hi, Maria. I just called to say hello.
MARIA:	Oh, hi, Yolanda.
YOLANDA:	What's the matter? You sound depressed.
MARIA:	Well, every time the phone rings, I think it might be Igor Kessler.
YOLANDA:	Haven't you heard anything yet?
MARIA:	No, no news yet. I've already called his office twice, but he wasn't in.
YOLANDA:	He probably hasn't even looked at your designs. I'm sure he's very busy.
MARIA:	I sent him my best work. But I'm really nervous. This is such a great opportunity.

2

YOLANDA:	I'm sure you're going to have a lot of opportunities. You're very talented.
MARIA:	I know. But Kessler is the most famous designer in New York.
YOLANDA:	Maria, I'm sorry. Can I call you back? Someone's at the door.
MARIA:	Sure. Talk to you later.

3

MARIA:	That was fast, Yolanda.
SECRETARY:	Excuse me?
MARIA:	Oh, I'm sorry. Who's this?
SECRETARY:	I'm calling from Igor Kessler's studio. May I speak to Maria Gorska?
MARIA:	Oh. Yes. This is Maria Gorska!

2 Answer the questions.

1. Why did Yolanda call?
2. How did Maria sound when Yolanda called?
3. Why did Yolanda hang up the phone?
4. Who was the second phone call from?

3 Warm Up

Your classmate has a problem. Ask what's wrong.

A: What's the matter?
B: I'm *nervous about my interview.*
A: Don't worry. I'm sure *you'll do fine.*

DEVELOP YOUR VOCABULARY

concerned	apprehensive
anxious	. . .
uptight	

Practice

A.

Has Maria **typed** a new résumé **yet?**	Yes, she did it this morning.
Maria **has already finished** her new dress. She finished it yesterday.	
She **hasn't picked up** her coat **yet.** Her sister's going to do it.	

1 Maria is going to have an interview with Igor Kessler. She has a lot of things to do before the interview, so she made a list. Listen and check the things she has already done.

2 Now look at Maria's list and say what she has already done and what she hasn't done yet.

Maria has already *finished her new dress.*
She hasn't *picked up her coat from the cleaners* yet.

TO DO

✓ finish dress design
pick up coat from cleaners
polish shoes
iron blouse
get a haircut
type new résumé
talk to art teacher
about Kessler

3 Look at the pictures and talk about them with a classmate.

1. A: Has Yolanda's aunt left the hospital yet?
   B: No, she hasn't.

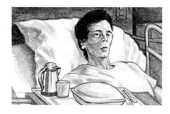

1. Yolanda's aunt / leave hospital

2. the police / find Janet Garvey

3. the Carsons / start trip

4. Yolanda / eat dinner

5. Dave / drive new truck

6. Roberto's band / perform at Jazzland

4 **Make a list of things you have to do every week. Exchange lists with a classmate. Then find out what your classmate has already done.**

A: Have you *done your laundry* yet?
B: Yes, I have. I *did it yesterday.*
   OR   No, I haven't. I'm going to *do it tomorrow.*

Student A can use these ideas:

do your homework	do your housecleaning
go shopping	go to the bank
pay your bills	

B.

kind → kind**est** nasty → nast**iest**	Igor Kessler is **the kindest** man in the world. Pierre Caché is **the nastiest** man I've ever met.
famous → **most** famous	Igor Kessler is **the most famous** designer in New York.
good → **best** bad → **worst**	Maria sent Kessler **her best** designs. She didn't show him **her worst** ones.

1 **Maria is at Igor Kessler's studio waiting for her interview. She is speaking to a man in the waiting room. Complete their conversation with the correct superlative form of the adjectives.**

MAN: Where did you study?

MARIA: At the Manhattan School of Design. How about you?

MAN: I studied with Pierre Caché in Paris.

MARIA: Pierre Caché! What's he like?

MAN: He's the *nastiest*, _____ man I've ever met, but he's also the
              1. nasty   2. egotistical
    _____ designer I've ever worked with.
     3. good

MARIA: I've heard that Igor Kessler is very nice. My art teacher is one of his

    _____ friends, and she says he's one of the _____ people she knows.
      4. old   5. kind

MAN: But he's also one of the _____. Your work has to be perfect.
                         6. demanding

MARIA: This is the _____ interview of my life. I hope it's not going to be my
              7. important

_____.
8. bad

2 Review and Build

Here are four of the designs that Maria showed Igor Kessler. What do you think of them? Talk about them like this:

A: I think design *A* is *more beautiful* than design *D*.
B: In my opinion, design *C* is the *strangest*.
C: Design *B* looks *comfortable*.

DEVELOP YOUR VOCABULARY

attractive	pretty
casual	simple
dressy	sporty
elegant	. . .

a   b   c   d

3 Talk about jobs.

A: I'd like to be *a teacher*. It's not the *most lucrative* job, but it's the *most rewarding*.
B: I think I'd like to be *a computer operator*. It's not the *most interesting* job, but it's the *most secure*.

DEVELOP YOUR VOCABULARY

challenging	glamorous
stimulating	creative
. . .	

PUT IT ALL TOGETHER

1 Listen to Maria and Dave's conversation. Then read these letters. Which one did Maria receive?

Kessler Fashion Designs
1328 Broadway
New York, NY 10018

July 7, 1988

Ms. Maria Gorska
27 W. 76 Street, Apt. 4–B
New York, NY 10023

Dear Maria,

Congratulations on getting the job! I'm very glad you're going to be working with me. Your art teacher told me that you were her most talented student, and she was certainly right. See you at the studio.

Igor Kessler

1

Kessler Fashion Designs
1328 Broadway
New York, NY 10018

July 7, 1988

Ms. Maria Gorska
27 W. 76 Street, Apt. 4–B
New York, NY 10023

Dear Maria,

I'm sorry to tell you that I have chosen a more experienced designer for the assistant designer's position. I know you are going to be very disappointed, but you shouldn't give up. You are one of the most talented young designers I've met. I'm sure you are going to be successful.

Sincerely,

Igor Kessler

2

Kessler Fashion Designs
1328 Broadway
New York, NY 10018

July 7, 1988

Ms. Maria Gorska
27 W. 76 Street, Apt. 4–B
New York, NY 10023

Dear Ms. Gorska:

This letter is to inform you that we cannot offer you the position of assistant designer. Thank you for your interest in Kessler Fashion Designs.

Sincerely,

Doris Strauss

Doris Strauss
Head Designer

3

---

2 Now listen to Dave and Maria's conversation again and answer the questions.

1. What is Maria's news?
2. What does Dave say when he hears her news?
3. What does he say to make Maria feel better?

Now roleplay a similar situation.
Student A tells Student B some bad news.
Student B says he or she is sorry and says something encouraging like this:

A: My son failed his math test.
B: I'm sorry to hear that. I'm sure he'll do better next time.

Student A can use these ideas:

> didn't get a raise (promotion)
> got fired
> broke up with a girlfriend (boyfriend)

ON YOUR OWN
Discuss these questions with your classmates.

1 Imagine you have a job interview. What do you do before the interview?

2 What types of questions can an interviewer ask you? What questions *can't* an interviewer ask you? What kinds of questions can *you* ask the interviewer?

— *Reading*

1 Vocabulary building. Before you read this article, complete the sentences with the correct answer.

1. Mary is <u>out of work.</u> She
   a. needs a job.
   b. left the house and went to work.

2. If your résumé is <u>up to date,</u>
   a. you should write a new one.
   b. it has the most recent information about you.

3. A friend gave me <u>a tip</u> about finding a job. She gave me some
   a. advice.
   b. money.

4. My friend has been out of work for six months. He wants to <u>keep looking,</u> so he
   a. is not going to stop trying to find a job.
   b. has decided he can't find a job.

YOU Magazine

WANTED: THE RIGHT JOB

You have been out of work for six months. You want to find a job but have had no success. What should you do? Take our Job Hunting Skills Quiz and you can answer that question for yourself.

Success starts with a good interview

TEST YOUR JOB HUNTING SKILLS

1. **Before you started to look for work, did you answer the question, "What do I really want to do?"**
   a) Yes.
   b) I thought about it a little.
   c) I never thought about it.

2. **Have you prepared an up-to-date résumé?**
   a) Yes.
   b) I have a résumé, but it's two years old.
   c) I don't have a résumé.

3. **Have you called all your friends, relatives, neighbors and classmates and told them you are looking for work? Do you read the help-wanted ads?**
   a) Yes.
   b) I read the ads, but I haven't called my friends.
   c) Someone should call *me.*

4. **When you send your résumé to a company, do you address it to a specific person, not just "Dear Sir or Madam"?**
   a) Yes.
   b) I usually send it to a specific person or to the Personnel Department.
   c) I just send it to the company.

5. **Do you send a short thank-you note after each interview? (This is your chance to remind the person you spoke to about your qualifications.)**
   a) Yes.
   b) I've sent notes, but haven't mentioned my qualifications.
   c) I've never sent thank-you notes.

(continued)

(continued)

HOW TO SCORE YOUR QUIZ

- 10 points for each "a" answer.
- 5 points for each "b" answer.
- 0 for each "c" answer.

If you scored between 40 and 50, just keep looking—your luck is sure to change soon.

If you scored between 15 and 40, try some of the tips in the quiz.

If you scored less than 15, follow the advice in the quiz carefully.

THE MOST IMPORTANT ADVICE

It is important to:

- know what you want
- have an up-to-date résumé
- tell everyone you know about your job search
- send your résumé to a specific person, not just to "Dear Sir or Madam." If a company has a Personnel Department, you can send your cover letter and résumé there. If not, you can call the company to find the name of the person you should send your résumé to.
- follow your interview with a polite thank-you note.

But the most important advice is—Don't give up! The right job for you is out there somewhere, and if you keep trying, you can find it.

2 Using what you've learned. Mary is talking to a friend about her job search. She is doing several things wrong. What should she do?

1. "I don't know what kind of job I want."

Mary should decide what she wants to do.

2. "Yes, I have a résumé. I wrote it two years ago, before I graduated from school."

3. "No, I don't want my friends to know I'm not working."

4. "Yes, I sent my résumé to the telephone company. But I didn't send it to a specific person."

5. "Why should I thank him for the interview? That's his job!"

3 Put the following steps in the right order.

1. Write a brief thank-you note for the interview.
2. Prepare a résumé.
3. Go to an interview.
4. Send the résumé to companies.
5. Read want ads and tell friends about your job search.
6. Answer the question, "What do I really want to do?"

*Writing*

Skill: Summarizing and putting events in order
Task: Writing a résumé

Your résumé introduces you and gives a summary of your work experience and training.

1 Study the résumé:

	Sonia Marino	Name, address and phone number at top
	126 Monroe Street	
	Hazelton, Iowa 50641	
	(319) 326–7727	
Experience:	Toddler Time, Inc.	List your most recent experience first.
1983 to present	250 Main St., Hazelton, Iowa	
	Design clothing for children.	
	Work on shows with manager.	
1981 to 1983	Baby Snooks, Inc.	Start sentences with verbs that describe your responsibilities: design, sell, assist, etc.
	25 10th Ave., Iowa Falls, Iowa	
	Sold children's clothing.	
	Assisted head buyer.	
Education:	Downtown Technical Academy	No diplomas? Then list special training programs . . .
1983	Des Moines, Iowa	
	Certificate of Clothing Design	
Honors:	First Prize in Johnstone Corp.	awards, and . . .
1983	children's clothing design competition	
Personal Interests:	Amateur Theater	community activities. Personal information should relate to the job you want.
	Design sets and costumes for local YWCA children's theater.	

2 Now prepare and write your own résumé.

1. Start with your name, address and telephone number.
2. Now list your work experience. Put your most recent experience first, then your next most recent, etc.

   Many people have little or no work experience. If so, start with your education and training, and give your work experience next. You should include training and experience you received in the military.
3. If you started with work experience, education comes next. Again, put the most recent program or degree first.
4. Now list any honors or special awards (most recent first).
5. Finally, list your hobbies.

3 Your last step is to check over your résumé carefully. Remember—your résumé introduces you, and it should look good.

For pronunciation exercises for Unit 11, see page 113.

12 Looking at the Future

1 Dave and Maria are at a street fair. Listen to their conversation.

1

DAVE: Oh, look, Maria! Have you ever been to a fortune teller?

MARIA: No. I don't believe in that stuff.

DAVE: Oh, come on! It'll be fun. Wouldn't you like to know your future?

MARIA: OK. But please don't tell anyone.

DAVE: Don't worry. No one will know.

2

VERA: Just ask me what you want to know.

DAVE: OK. Will anything exciting happen to me this year?

VERA: Let's see. Ah, yes. You will take a trip to somewhere warm.

DAVE: That sounds good. Will I go alone?

VERA: No, you won't. You will go with someone special—a woman, I think.

3

VERA: And what would *you* like to ask?

MARIA: Will anything bad happen to me this year?

VERA: No, nothing bad will happen, but something wonderful will happen. Perhaps you will marry this young man.

MARIA: But I've only known him since April!

VERA: Sometimes love is like that, Maria.

MARIA: Maria! How did you know my name?

VERA: I've been a fortune teller for a long time.

2 Answer the questions.

1. Was it Maria's idea to go to the fortune teller?
2. Will Dave take a trip?
3. Will Maria marry Dave?
4. Why was Maria surprised at the end?

3 Warm Up

Ask a classmate about his or her future.

A: Will you ever *go back to China?*

B: Yes, I will. I hope to *go back next year.*
   OR   I don't think so. *I'll probably stay here.*

DEVELOP YOUR VOCABULARY

In the

spring   summer   fall   winter

Practice

A.

How long has Maria **known** Dave?	She**'s known** him	**since** April. **for** three months.

Use *for* with a period of time.

for	an hour two days three weeks five years a long time

Use *since* with a definite time.

since	9 A.M. August 17 yesterday last week 1985 I moved to New York

1 **The fortune teller told Dave a lot about his life. Look at the pictures and make statements with *for* and *since*.**

1. Dave has lived in New York for six years.

1. live / six years

2. be / last February

3. play drums / 1982

4. know Maria / three months

5. have new truck / six weeks

6. like baseball / a long time

2 Maria talked to Vera the fortune teller for a long time. Listen to their conversation and answer the questions.

1. How long has Vera been a fortune teller?
2. How long has Vera had visions of the future?
3. How long has Maria studied art?
4. How long has Vera been at the street fair today?

3 Find out more about a classmate's life.

A: How long have you *lived in the United States?*
B: I've *been here since 1985.*

You can use these words:

be	own
have	speak
know	study

B.

> Will **anything*** bad happen?
> No. **Something*** wonderful will happen.
> **Everything** will be great.
>
> The fortune teller didn't say **anything** bad.
> She said **nothing** bad.

-body	-one	-where	-thing
somebody	someone	somewhere	something
anybody	anyone	anywhere	anything
nobody	no one	nowhere	nothing
everybody	everyone	everywhere	everything

Note: Remember, we usually use *any* in questions and negative sentences. We use *some* in affirmative sentences.

1 Read these questions and complete the answers with an appropriate word from the box above.

1. A: What did Dave want?

   B: He wanted ___*somebody*___ to tell his fortune.

2. A: Did the fortune teller say anything bad about Maria or Dave?

   B: No, she said _____ bad.

3. A: Did the fortune teller know a lot about Maria?

   B: Yes. She knew almost _____ about her.

4. A: What will happen to Maria?

   B: She will marry _____ terrific.

5. A: What will happen to Dave?

   B: He will go _____ with a woman.

6. A: Did the fortune teller say anything about Yolanda?

   B: No. She didn't say _____ about her.

2 Invite a classmate to the movies.

A: Would you like to go the movies tonight?

B: Yes. But let's not see anything *scary.*

A: How about something *with Clint Eastwood?*

B: That sounds fine.

    OR   I'd rather see something *light.*

DEVELOP YOUR VOCABULARY

amusing	funny
depressing	heavy
dubbed	serious
foreign	. . .

C.

Dave **will take** a trip.	
Will he **go** alone?	No, he **won't.**
Where **will** he **go?**	He**'ll go** somewhere warm.

I will	=	I'll
it will	=	it'll
she will	=	she'll
they will	=	they'll
will not	=	won't

1 Dave is talking to Steve on the telephone. Listen to their conversation and complete it. Use contractions when you hear them.

STEVE: Can I borrow your typewriter, Dave?

DAVE: Sure. You can come and get it tomorrow.

STEVE: <u>Will</u> _____ be home tonight?
       1   2

DAVE: _____ _____ be home before 11:00. _____ be out with Maria.
      3   4   5

STEVE: Maria again, huh? Sounds serious. Are you two . . .?

DAVE: Don't worry. _____ tell you if we decide to get married.
                      6

STEVE: I think you should marry her. _____ be good for you.
                                 7

DAVE: _____ _____ even talk about it. She says it's too soon.
      8   9

STEVE: Oh, _____ change her mind.
         10

2 Look at the pictures and talk about these people's futures. Use *will*.

Dave and Maria will get married. Barbara will . . .

3 Find out where a classmate will be at a certain time.

A: Where will you be *tomorrow at 5:00?*
B: I'll be *home*. What about you?
A: I'll be *at work*.

4 Make predictions about the future by completing these sentences.

1. I think people in the future will . . .
2. In my opinion, scientists will . . .
3. It's possible that children won't . . .
4. Perhaps there won't be any . . .
5. Maybe there'll be more . . .

Now make some more predictions.

Housing

1 **Maria and Dave are going to get married. They found an apartment and are going to sign a lease. Look at the first part of their lease.**

LEASE AGREEMENT

The Landlord and Tenant agree to lease the Apartment for the Term and at the Rent stated on these terms:

LANDLORD:
Wykart Apartments
Address for Notices 3812 Riverside Drive
N.Y., N.Y. 10025

TENANT:
David Carson
Maria Gorska

Apartment (and terrace, if any) 5-F at 400 W. 85th Street, N.Y., N.Y. 10024
Bank

| Lease date:
November 15, 1988 | Term 2 years
beginning December 1. 1988
ending December 1 1990 | Yearly Rent $6,300
Monthly Rent $ 525.00
Security $ 525.00 |

Broker*

Rider Additional terms on .... page(s) initialed at the end by the parties is attached and made a part of this Lease.

Use The Apartment must be used only as a private   Landlord is allowed to keep for expenses. Landlord need

Now read each sentence and choose the correct answer.

1. A *lease* is a type of ___*Contract*___.
   contract / apartment / letter

2. The person who owns the building is called the

   _____.
   tenant / landlord / manager

3. The people who will live at 400 W. 85th Street are called the

   _____.
   landlords / tenants / neighbors

4. The money you pay every month to live in an apartment is called the

   _____.
   term / rent / security

5. Maria and Dave have to pay $525 every _____.
   year / month / week

6. Maria and Dave can move into this apartment on

   _____.
   November 15, 1988 / December 1, 1988 / December 1, 1989

7. This lease is good for _____ year(s).
   one / two / three

8. This lease expires* in _____.
   1988 / 1989 / 1990

* = comes to an end

For Your Information

Security deposits

Before you move into a new apartment, you have to pay a *security deposit* to the owner (landlord). This protects the owner against damage to the apartment. When you move out, the owner has to return the money to you if the apartment is in good condition and if you have paid all of your rent.

2 Dave has some questions about the lease. He is talking with the building manager. Listen to their conversation and check the correct column.

Who will . . .

	The Tenant	The Landlord
1. put the security deposit in the bank?		✓
2. get the interest on the security deposit?		
3. pay for the gas?		
4. pay for the electricity?		
5. arrange for a new telephone?		
6. paint the apartment?		
7. provide exterminating service?		

3 Now ask a classmate questions like these about his or her home. Use the ideas in Exercise 2.

Who pays for electricity?
Does your landlord provide exterminating service?
. . .

4 Dave and Maria are looking at their apartment. They notice some problems. Match each sentence with its picture.

1. _e_ The kitchen faucet is leaking.
2. ____ The paint is peeling.
3. ____ A window is broken.
4. ____ There's not enough heat.
5. ____ The chain lock is broken.
6. ____ Something is wrong with the toilet.
7. ____ There are bugs in the kitchen.

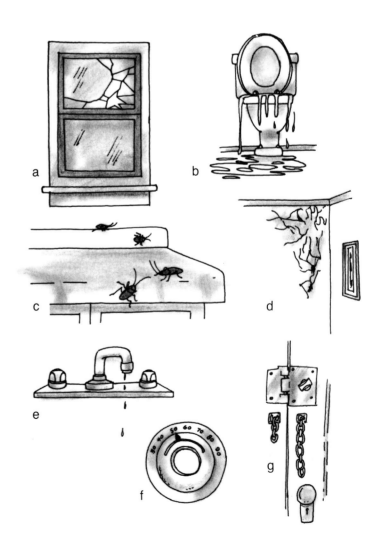

5 Maria called the landlord's office to complain about some of the problems. Listen to her conversation with the building manager and complete it.

MANAGER: Wykart Apartments.

MARIA: Hello, this is ___Maria___ ₁ ___Gorska___ ₂. I'm a new _____ ₃ at _____ ₄ _____ ₅ _____ ₆ _____ ₇.

MANAGER: What's your _____ ₈ _____ ₉?

MARIA: It's _____ ₁₀.

MANAGER: Yes. Now how can I help you?

MARIA: I have a _____ ₁₁ with my _____ ₁₂ _____ ₁₃. It's _____ ₁₄.

MANAGER: OK. We'll take care of it.

MARIA: There's also _____ ₁₅ wrong with my _____ ₁₆. It's very noisy.

MANAGER: I'm sorry. That's not our responsibility.

MARIA: Oh? Well, _____ ₁₇ anyway.

MANAGER: _____ ₁₈.

MARIA: Bye. Hmm. I'm going to _____ ₁₉ _____ ₂₀ more about that!

Now roleplay a similar situation. Call your landlord's office to complain about a problem. Use your own information.

For Your Information

Landlord-tenant problems

Sometimes your landlord may refuse to make a repair or may take too long to repair something. Sometimes you may not get enough heat or hot water. If you have a problem with your landlord, you can get help from several organizations. To find out who to contact in your city, call City Hall or the Legal Aid Society.

Just for Fun

6 There are five problems in this kitchen. Can you find them?

ON YOUR OWN

Think about Maria and Dave's experience with the fortune teller. Then discuss these questions with your classmates.

1 Do you believe in fortune tellers? Did you ever go to one? If so, what happened?

2 Imagine you are with a fortune teller. What questions would you like to ask?

For pronunciation exercises for Unit 12, see page 113.

REVIEW 6

1 Look at Dave and Maria's list of things to do before they get married. Say what they *have already done* and what they *haven't done yet*.

They've already signed the lease.
They haven't cleaned Dave's old apartment yet.

> *To Do*
> ✓ sign lease for new apartment
> clean Dave's old apartment
> ✓ speak to building manager
> buy bed
> buy couch
> ✓ get a new telephone
> ✓ find a moving company
> invite Yolanda and Roberto for dinner

2 Ask questions about these people. Use *yet* and the present perfect.

1. A: (Maria and Dave) *Have Maria and Dave gotten married yet?*
   B: No, they're going to get married next month.
2. A: (Steve and Julie) _____
   B: No, they're still living in their old apartment.
3. A: (Maria) _____
   B: Yes, she had the interview last week.
4. A: (the Carsons) _____
   B: Yes, they arrived in Madrid on June 6.
5. A: (Los Santos) _____
   B: No. They're going to make their record next month.
6. A: (the police) _____
   B: No, they're still looking for Janet Garvey.

3 Complete this conversation. Use the superlative form of the adjectives.

YOLANDA: Tell me about your new apartment, Maria.

MARIA: Well, it's not the _biggest_ one we saw, but I think it's the _____.
1. big   2. nice

YOLANDA: What's the _____ thing about it?
3. good

MARIA: The rent. It was the _____ of all the ones we saw. The _____ thing
4. cheap   5. bad

about it is the size. But even the _____ apartment we saw was also small.
6. expensive

YOLANDA: Well, the _____ thing is that you and Dave will have your own place. I'm
7. important

sure it'll be one of the _____ times in your life.
8. happy

MARIA: I am too. Dave is the _____ man I've ever known.
9. wonderful

4 Complete these sentences. Use *for* or *since*.

1. Maria has known Dave __since__ April.
2. Dave's parents have been married _____ a long time.
3. Dave has lived in New York _____ six years.
4. Yolanda has made jewelry _____ she was a young girl.
5. Maria has had the flu _____ weeks.
6. Barbara has been blind _____ she was born.

5 Ask questions. Use the present perfect of an appropriate verb.

1. How long / this country.

How long have you been in this country?

2. How long / English
3. How long / this class
4. How long / the other students
5. How long / *(your occupation)*
6. How long / this English book

Now answer the questions. Use your own information.

6 Match the questions in column A with the answers in column B.

A	B
1. _b_ Who did Dave tell?	a. Somewhere special.
2. ____ What did you do last night?	b. Nobody. It was a secret.
3. ____ What did you have for dinner?	c. Everything. It was great.
4. ____ Where did you go last weekend?	d. Something delicious.
5. ____ What did you like about the movie?	e. There isn't anything in the refrigerator.
6. ____ What's the matter?	f. Nothing. I just stayed home.

7 Complete these sentences. Use *will*, *'ll* or *won't* and the verbs.

1. A: Is Maria home?

    B: No, but she *'ll be* home in an hour.
       _{be}

2. A: _____ Dave _____ his parents in
             _{visit}

    Europe?

    B: No, he _____.

3. A: _____ Steve and Julie _____ to
             _{move}

    Chicago?

    B: No, they _____ in New York.
             _{stay}

4. A: Hasn't Ricky done his homework yet?

    B: No, but he _____ it later.
             _{do}

5. A: Can you call me tomorrow?

    B: Sure. I _____ you at noon.
             _{call}

6. A: _____ Dave and Maria

    _____ married?
       _{get}

    B: Yes, they _____.

7. A: _____ it _____ tomorrow?
               _{rain}

    B: No, I think it _____ nice.
               _{be}

Pronunciation

The Pronunciation exercises are recorded on cassette after the listening exercises for each unit. The Tapescripts are found at the back of the Teacher's Manual.

UNIT 1

Part 1

A. Listen and write the numbers of the words that have a vowel sound like the *a* in *name*.

1. paid
2. hate
3. say
4. table
5. mad
6. game
7. wash
8. hat
9. made
10. cane
11. day
12. neighbor
13. part
14. pad
15. great
16. eight
17. can
18. start

Listen again and repeat the words that have a vowel sound like the *a* in *name*.

B. Listen and repeat these sentences.

1. She works as a waitress every day.
2. They're playing a card game at the table.
3. What's your neighbor's name?

C. Look at Exercise A. What is the sound of these letters? –a–e –ai– –ay –ei– –ea–

Part 2

A. Words in English have stress on different syllables. Many words have stress on the first syllable. Listen and repeat these words.

1. market
2. T-shirt
3. waitress
4. restaurant
5. washable
6. worker
7. factory
8. jewelry
9. taxi
10. driver

B. Listen and repeat these phrases.

1. T-shirt painter
2. part-time waitress
3. taxi driver
4. jewelry maker
5. street market
6. factory worker
7. fast-food restaurant
8. washable T-shirts

UNIT 2

Part 1

A. Listen and write the numbers of the words that have a vowel sound like the *o* in *no*.

1. won't
2. cot
3. grocery
4. home
5. want
6. coat
7. store
8. soda
9. stole
10. come
11. not
12. know
13. don't
14. those
15. does
16. only

Listen again and repeat the words that have a vowel sound like the *o* in *no*.

B. Listen and repeat these sentences.

1. Janet stole the expensive stone.
2. Buy a soda at the grocery store.
3. Who broke the window?
4. We drove the boys home.

C. Look at Exercise A. What is the sound of these letters? –o–e –ow –oa–

Part 2

A. Some words in English have stress on the second syllable. Listen and repeat these words.

1. about
2. computer
3. delicious
4. tomorrow
5. around
6. machine
7. department
8. design
9. today

B. Listen and repeat these phrases.

1. expensive machines
2. about computers
3. around the department
4. today and tomorrow

UNIT 3

Part 1

A. Listen. Which word do you hear—*a.* or *b.?*

1. a. it   b. eat
2. a. chip   b. cheap
3. a. live   b. leave
4. a. sit   b. seat
5. a. fit   b. feet
6. a. still b. steal

Now listen again and repeat each word.

B. Listen and repeat these sentences.

1. She didn't see it.
2. Please give me a little bit.
3. The police are still looking for the thief.

C. Look at Exercise A. What is the sound of these letters? –ee– –ea–
What is the sound of this letter? –i–

Part 2

A. Some words in English have stress on the third syllable. Listen and repeat these words.

1. conversàtion   3. composìtion   5. understànd
2. afternòon   4. reservàtion   6. introdùce

B. Listen and repeat these phrases.

1. màke the reservàtion
2. wrìte the composìtion
3. understànd the conversàtion
4. wait until the afternòon

UNIT 4

Part 1

A. Listen and write the numbers of the words that have a vowel sound like the *i* in *like*.

1. time   4. drive   7. living   9. begin
2. list   5. night   8. thin   10. fine
3. high   6. five

Listen again and repeat the words that have a vowel sound like the *i* in *like*.

B. Listen and repeat these sentences.

1. Steve arrived at night.
2. Dave likes to begin on time.
3. She got her driver's license.

C. Look at Exercise A. What is the sound of these letters? –i–e –igh–
What is the sound of this letter? –i–

Part 2

A. Listen to these words and mark the stressed syllable in each one.

Example: reservàtion

1. appreciate   5. necklace   9. performer
2. explain   6. yesterday   10. mechanic
3. holiday   7. identify   11. favorite
4. application   8. probably   12. umbrella

Now listen again and repeat the words.

B. Listen and repeat these sentences.

1. That's my favorite holiday.
2. Did Yolanda identify the thief yesterday?
3. The mechanic explained the problem.
4. I lost my umbrella and my necklace.

UNIT 5

Part 1

A. Listen and write the numbers of the words that have the same vowel sound as *few*.

1. cube   3. put   5. use   7. future   9. but
2. excuse   4. wood   6. mule   8. beauty   10. view

Listen again and repeat the words that have the same vowel sound as *few*.

B. Listen and repeat these sentences.

1. He is a Cuban musician.
2. What a beautiful view!
3. I can't excuse you in the future.

C. Look at Exercise A. What is the sound of these letters? –u–e

Part 2

A. Vowels in unstressed syllables are usually pronounced /ə/ or /ɪ/. Listen to these words and cross out the unstressed vowel sounds.

Example: markẹt

1. again   4. questions   7. started   10. immigrant
2. teaches   5. forget   8. famous   11. fashion
3. design   6. arrive   9. correct   12. magazine

Now listen again and repeat the words.

B. Listen and repeat these sentences.

1. He teaches design.
2. I started to answer the questions.
3. That fashion magazine is famous.

UNIT 6

Part 1

A. Which word do you hear—*a.* or *b.*?

1. a. man   b. men   4. a. band   b. bend
2. a. bat   b. bet   5. a. sat   b. set
3. a. bad   b. bed   6. a. tan   b. ten

Now listen again and repeat each word.

B. Listen and repeat these sentences.

1. Yolanda knows the men in the band.
2. I want a hamburger with ketchup and lettuce.
3. Thank you for the tennis racket.

C. Look at Exercise A. What is the sound of this letter? –e–
What is the sound of this letter? –a–

(continued)

Part 2

A. Sometimes an unstressed syllable is reduced so much it disappears. The following words have more syllables than we usually pronounce. Listen to them and cross out the letters that you *don't* hear.

Example: natᴜral

1. interesting
2. different
3. references
4. comfortable
5. temperature
6. vegetable

Now listen again and repeat each word.

B. Listen and repeat these sentences.

1. New York is an interesting city.
2. This is a comfortable temperature.
3. I need different references.

UNIT 7

Part 1

A. Listen. Which word do you hear—*a.* or *b.*?

1. a. map   b. mop
2. a. hat   b. hot
3. a. Nat   b. not
4. a. jab   b. job
5. a. tap   b. top
6. a. cat   b. cot

Now listen again and repeat each word.

B. Listen and repeat these sentences.

1. Put the hat on top of the box.
2. Mom got the job.
3. Steve did not win the lottery.

C. Look at Exercise A. What is the sound of this letter?   –a–
   What is the sound of this letter?   –o–

Part 2

Listen to these phrases and mark the stressed syllables.

Example: win the lottery

1. fantastic promotion
2. nervous doctor
3. million dollars
4. lots of money
5. take a vacation
6. newspaper reporter

Now listen again and repeat the phrases.

UNIT 8

Part 1

A. Listen and write the numbers of the words that have a vowel sound like the *u* in *bus.*

1. book
2. money
3. look
4. truck
5. much
6. doesn't
7. wonderful
8. took
9. up
10. luck
11. does
12. good

Listen again and repeat the words that have a vowel sound like the *u* in *bus.*

B. Listen and repeat these sentences.

1. He got a wonderful truck.
2. The bus doesn't cost much money.
3. Wish me good luck.

Part 2

Words in English have stressed syllables, and sentences have stressed words. Listen to these sentences and mark the stressed words.

Example: Do you know what they got you?

1. They're going to surprise me.
2. Of course, it's yours!
3. Did you get your check yet?
4. We're glad you like it.

Now listen again and repeat the sentences.

UNIT 9

Part 1

A. Listen and write the numbers of the words that have a vowel sound like the *a* in *call.*

1. tall
2. cut
3. caught
4. done
5. dog
6. wrong
7. lunch
8. audition
9. lucky
10. bought
11. fall
12. but

Listen again and repeat the words that have a vowel sound like the *a* in *call.*

B. Listen and repeat these sentences.

1. His audition was wonderful.
2. Call the lawyer during lunch.
3. They were exhausted after they caught the boy.

Part 2

Listen to these sentences and mark the word that has the *most* stress in each sentence.

Example: We can't call now.

1. It's too late.
2. She doesn't go to bed this early.
3. I think we can call.
4. It is very important.
5. But it's not definite.
6. You're going to be very famous.
7. Not too famous, I hope.

Now listen again and repeat the sentences.

UNIT 10

Part 1

A. Listen and write the numbers of the words that have a vowel sound like the *ou* in *out*.

1. awful	4. mouth	7. call	10. fall
2. now	5. ought	8. foul	11. month
3. cough	6. cow	9. bought	12. plow

Now listen again and repeat the words that have a vowel sound like the *ou* in *out*.

B. Listen and repeat these sentences.

1. He looked at the cow's mouth.
2. You have to go out now.
3. Now is the time to call.

C. Look at Exercise A. What is the sound of these letters?   —ow—
In Exercise A, the letters   —ou—   have two different sounds. What are they?

Part 2

Listen to these sentences and mark the stressed words.

1. I've got an upset stomach.
2. They say it's really exciting.
3. Do you have a fever?
4. Have you taken any medicine?

Now listen again and repeat the sentences.

UNIT 11

Part 1

A. Listen and write the numbers of the words that have a vowel sound like the *oy* in *boy*.

1. toy	4. wood	7. joy
2. boil	5. suit	8. employ
3. play	6. soil	9. annoy

Listen again and repeat the words that have a vowel sound like the *oy* in *boy*.

B. Listen and repeat these sentences.

1. Boil the water.
2. I just bought a toy for the boy.
3. Don't annoy the little boy.

C. Look at Exercise A. What is the sound of these letters? —oi—   —oy—

Part 2

Sometimes we give special emphasis to some information by stressing it more than we usually do. Listen to this sentence with normal stress.

Kessler's the most famous designer in New York.

Now listen again.

KESSLER'S the most famous designer in New York. (Not *anyone* else.)

Now listen again.

Kessler's the most famous DESIGNER in New York. (Not *anything* else.)

Listen to the people talking. Then from the lists below, choose the correct sentence to finish the second person's answer.

1. a. I'm going to the movies.
   b. You're going to school.
   c. I'm leaving school.
2. a. I have an old one.
   b. You have a new one.
   c. I have a new truck.
3. a. He's at home.
   b. Steve is.
   c. Dave Campbell is.

UNIT 12

Part 1

A. Listen. Which word do you hear—*a.* or *b.*?

1. a. boot	b. but		4. a. dude	b. dud
2. a. soon	b. son		5. a. duke	b. duck
3. a. coop	b. cup		6. a. who	b. huh

Now listen again and repeat each word.

B. Listen and repeat these sentences.

1. Who drove the truck to the studio?
2. Julie saw her son.
3. It's too soon to do it.

C. Look at Exercise A. What is the sound of these letters?   —oo—   —u–e

Part 2

Listen to the two people talking. Then from the lists below, choose the correct sentence to finish the second person's answer.

1. a. She plays the violin.
   b. Barbara plays the flute.
   c. She plays the flute badly.
2. a. Maria doesn't.
   b. Maria likes fortune tellers.
   c. Dave likes street fairs.
3. a. Steve's going to get a new truck.
   b. Dave's going to get a new car.
   c. He's already got a new truck.

Irregular Verbs

Verb	Past Tense	Past Participle	Verb	Past Tense	Past Participle
be	was, were	been	lie	lay	lain
beat	beat	beaten	light	lit *or* lighted	lit *or* lighted
become	became	become	lose	lost	lost
begin	began	begun	make	made	made
bend	bent	bent	mean	meant	meant
bet	bet	bet	meet	met	met
bite	bit	bitten	pay	paid	paid
bleed	bled	bled	put	put	put
blow	blew	blown	read	read	read
break	broke	broken	ride	rode	ridden
bring	brought	brought	ring	rang	rung
build	built	built	rise	rose	risen
burst	burst	burst	run	ran	run
buy	bought	bought	say	said	said
catch	caught	caught	see	saw	seen
choose	chose	chosen	sell	sold	sold
come	came	come	send	sent	sent
cost	cost	cost	set	set	set
cut	cut	cut	shake	shook	shaken
dive	dove	dived	shoot	shot	shot
do	did	done	shut	shut	shut
draw	drew	drawn	sing	sang	sung
drink	drank	drunk	sink	sank	sunk
drive	drove	driven	sit	sat	sat
eat	ate	eaten	sleep	slept	slept
fall	fell	fallen	slide	slid	slid
feed	fed	fed	speak	spoke	spoken
feel	felt	felt	spend	spent	spent
find	found	found	spit	spat *or* spit	spat *or* spit
fly	flew	flown	spread	spread	spread
forget	forgot	forgotten	stand	stood	stood
forgive	forgave	forgiven	steal	stole	stolen
freeze	froze	frozen	stick	stuck	stuck
get	got	gotten	sting	stung	stung
give	gave	given	stink	stank *or* stunk	stunk
go	went	gone	sweep	swept	swept
grow	grew	grown	swim	swam	swum
have	had	had	swing	swung	swung
hear	heard	heard	take	took	taken
hide	hid	hidden	teach	taught	taught
hit	hit	hit	tear	tore	torn
hold	held	held	tell	told	told
hurt	hurt	hurt	think	thought	thought
keep	kept	kept	throw	threw	thrown
know	knew	known	understand	understood	understood
lay	laid	laid	wake	woke	woken
lead	led	led	wear	wore	worn
leave	left	left	win	won	won
lend	lent	lent	write	wrote	written
let	let	let			

Useful Vocabulary

Weights and Measures

English system*

Length
1 inch	=	2.54 centimeters
1 foot (12 inches)	=	0.305 meter
1 yard (3 feet)	=	0.914 meter
1 mile (5,280 feet)	=	1.609 kilometers

Weight
1 ounce**	=	28.350 grams
1 pound (16 ounces)**	=	0.454 kilogram
1 ton (2,000 pounds)**	=	907.18 kilograms
	=	0.907 metric ton

Capacity
1 cup	=	0.237 liter
1 pint (2 cups)	=	0.473 liter
1 quart (2 pints)	=	0.946 liter
1 gallon (4 quarts)	=	3.785 liters

Metric system

Length
1 centimeter	=	0.394 inch
1 meter	=	39.37 inches
	=	3.281 feet
	=	1.093 yards
1 kilometer	=	0.621 mile

Weight
1 gram	=	0.035 ounce
1 kilogram	=	2.205 pounds
1 metric ton	=	1.102 tons

Capacity
1 liter	=	4.227 cups
	=	2.113 pints
	=	1.057 quarts
	=	0.264 gallon

Temperature
Conversion formulas

Fahrenheit = 9/5 C + 32

Centigrade = 5/9 (F − 32)

Equivalents

Boiling point				
of water:	212	°F	=	100°C
Body temperature:	98.6	°F	=	37°C

Freezing point				
of water:	32	°F	=	0°C

*This is still the dominant system of measurement in the U.S., although the metric system has been introduced there. The metric system is now the official system of measurement in other English-speaking countries, although the English system is still used in everyday language.

**avoirdupois

USEFUL VOCABULARY

Clothes

Men's and Women's

belt
coat
gloves
hat
jacket
jeans
pants
scarf
shoes
shorts
sneakers
socks
suit
sweater
T-shirt

Men's

shirt
sports coat
tie

Underclothes

underwear (briefs, shorts)
undershirt

Women's

blouse
dress
purse
skirt

Underclothes

bra
pantyhose
slip
stockings
underwear (underpants)

Clothing sizes

Women's

	Blouses, dresses and suits						*Shoes*				
U.S.	8	10	12	14	16	18	5	6	7	8	9
Metric	38	40	42	44	46	48	35	36	37	38	39

Men's

	Shirts							*Shoes*					
U.S.	14	14½	15	15½	16	16½	17	7	8	9	10	11	12
Metric	36	37	38	39	41	42	43	40	41	42	43	44	45

Sports

baseball
basketball
bicycle riding
boxing
canoeing
diving
field hockey
fishing

football
gliding
golf
gymnastics
hang gliding
hockey
horseback riding
ice skating

polo
rowing
running
sailing
skating
skiing
soccer
surfing

swimming
table tennis
tennis
volleyball
water polo
water skiing
wind surfing
wrestling

Food

Meat, Poultry, Fish	Vegetables	Fruit	Dairy	Condiments
bacon	artichoke	apple	butter	honey
beef	asparagus	avocado	cheese	jam
cheeseburger	broccoli	banana	cream	jelly
chicken	cabbage	blueberry	egg	ketchup
duck	carrot	cherry	milk	mustard
fish	corn	grape		oil
goose	eggplant	grapefruit		pepper
ham	french fries	lemon	**Desserts**	salt
hamburger	garlic	mango		sugar
lamb	green beans	orange	cake	vinegar
pork	lettuce	papaya	chocolate	
tuna fish	onion	peach	cookie	
turkey	peas	pear	ice cream	**Beverages**
veal	potato	pineapple	pastry	
	salad	plum	pie	beer
	squash	raspberry	pudding	coffee
Other	tomato	strawberry		juice
				lemonade
bread				soda
cereal				tea
flour				water
ice				wine
potato chip				
pretzel				
rice				
soup				
spaghetti				

Word List _____

The numbers after each word indicate the page number where the word first appears. An asterisk (*) indicates the word is intended for recognition only on that page.

Words active in Student's Book 1 are not included in this list.

---

adj = adjective; *adv* = adverb; *aux* = auxiliary verb; *C* = on cassette;
conj = conjunction; *intrans* = intransitive verb; *n* = noun;
past part = past participle; *prep* = preposition; *pron* = pronoun;
s past = simple past tense; *trans* = transitive verb; *v* = verb

---

A
abstract *adj* 76
accept *88
accident *32
account 9
    account number 9
    checking account *70
    savings account 64
achy 82
across 10
ad: help-wanted ad *97
advantage *7
advice 97
afraid *32
after *conj* 40
after *prep*: run after 11
against: protect against
    *105
age *n* *13
agent *78
ago 21
agree 14
agreement 62
ahead: go ahead 38
airline 69
album (record) *26
    photo album 48
alcoholic *adj* 89
ale: ginger ale 51
all
    all the time *5C
    that's all *7
allergic reaction 89
already *76C, 92
also 2
ambitious 44
amount *70
amusing *adj* 103
anniversary 46
answer *n* 74
anxious 92
anybody 102
anymore 24

anyone 100
appliance 16
application form 43
appointment 88
    make an appointment
    88
appreciate 20
apprehensive 92
architect 41
argument 86
around *adv*
    joke around *4
    walk around 86
around *prep* 56
arrange for 106
arrest *v* 21
art 33
article (newspaper) *78C
as *conj*: as often as possible
    28
as *prep* 2
ask 100
assignment *45
assist 99
assistant *96
attractive 95
audience *78
audition *v* 74
away: right away 52
awful 14

B
back *adv*
    call back *24, 92
    get (something) back 20
back *n* (= reverse side) 71
bacon 47
bag
    camera bag 48
    sleeping bag 48
bake 67

baked 46
    baked beans 46
    baked potato 51
baking dish *49
ball 23
    bowling ball 48
    golf ball 48
    play ball 23
band (= musical group) 3
    rock band 20
Band-Aid 86
bandleader *41
bank teller 29
bar: snack bar 10
barbecue *n* 46
baseball
    baseball glove 48
    baseball player 41
basketball player 43
be: been 84
beans 46
    baked beans 46
    green beans 51
beard 13
beat *n* (in music) *79
beauty shop 69
became 56
bed *5C, 16
    go to bed *5C, 74
beef 46
been 84
beer 89
before *conj* 38
before *prep*: before long *44
beginning *n* 81
believe *44, 56
belt 17
bet: you bet *32
better *25, 64
    get better *30
beverage *51, 69
bicycle 23
bill *n* (money) 71

(from a store) 70
(restaurant check) *53
birth 70
    date of birth 70
birthday cake 46
blanket 16
blender 16
blew 11
blond 12
blow *v* 11
    blew 11
blue: once in a blue moon
    28
bookkeeper 29
boot 16
    hiking boot 48
boring *adj* 50
bottom 106
bowl *n* 51
bowling ball 48
boxing *n* *83C
bracelet 15
bread *89
break *n*: lucky break 74
break *v*
    broke *s past* 96
    break up (with a girl/
    boyfriend) 96
broccoli 46
broke *s past* 96
broken *adj* 69
brought *s past* 11
brown sugar 47
bug *n* 106
build *v* 67
    built *s past* 67
bullfight 27
bun 47
burn *n* 86
bus: take the bus 28
business deal *44
butter 52
buyer *99

ferry 27
festival 30
fever 82
few 38
fight n *26
filet of sole 51
filing clerk 21
finally *81
financial *78
finish v 9
fired: get fired 96
first-aid kit 48
flour 49
flower n 23
flu 82
fluid: lighter fluid 47
fly v *58C
folding chair 47
food 46
foot (pl feet) (measurement) 12
foreign 103
forget (to) 39
fork 52
form n (= kind) 70
    application form 43
fortune (wealth) *44
    fortune teller 100
freezer *66
french-fried potato 51
fried 51
frightened adj 42
front: in front *78
full time 38
    full-time 38
funny 103

G
gather intrans 79
generally 6
generous 64
get
    got 64
    get a haircut 93
    get (something) back 20
    get better *30
    get fired 96
    get off 35
    have got 46
ginger ale 51
give up *98
glad *50, 64
glamorous 95
glasses 13
    safety glasses 87
glove: baseball glove 48
go
    gone past part 84
    go ahead 38
    go on a picnic 22
    go sightseeing 27

go swimming 6
go to bed *5C, 74
go to jail 21
go window shopping *63
gold adj 15
golf ball 48
gone past part 84
good: make good *79
goodness: thank goodness *93C
got 64
    have got 46
graduate v 43
graduation 46
grass 75
green
    green beans 51
    green card 56
grill n 47
grilled adj 51
grin n *61
grocery store 10
ground meat 47
group n *61
grow old *26
guitarist *79

H
had past part 84
hair 13
haircut 93
    get a haircut 93
hall: music hall 33
hang up *92
happen 56
hard adj (= difficult) 38
    adv *41
hate v 30
have aux 82
    had past part 84
    have a good time 28
    have a party 46
    have friends over 6
    have got 46
    have the chance 28
    have time 38
hazel 13
head adj (most important) *96
head n: head of the family *44
health 87
    health clinic *88
hear *78, 92
    heard past part 92
heart: change of heart 79
heat n 106
heavy (= serious) 103
height *13
help out *5C
help-wanted ad *97

hers 68
hiking boot 48
his pron 68
hit n (= success) 26
hit v: hit it off 79
holiday 28
homesick 42
honey 86
honor n *99
hope (to) *25, 39
hot dog 46
housecleaning 94
    do the housecleaning 94
housewares 16
housewarming party 46
how?
    how about? 2
    how often? 7
    how tall? 12
hug v *61
hunting: job hunting *97

I
ice 86
    ice cream 51
identify 21
if so *7
ill 74
immediately *57
immigrant *41
in
    in fact 20
    in front *78
    in the past 24
inch 12
income 88
inconvenient *81
incredible *60C, 64
industry *44
inform *96
ingredient *49
inside adv 10
insurance 88
interest n (attention) *96
    (money) 102
interested adj *4
interview v *45
interviewer *43
invite 46
iron v 40
itinerary *58, 68

J
jail n 21
    go to jail 21
jar n 49
jelly 49
jewelry 3
    jewelry making *5C
job hunting *97
join trans *44
joke around *4
juice 49

jump rope v 23
junior 16
just (= recently) 56

K
keep (= continue) *61, 97
ketchup 47
kilogram 12
kind adj 94
kind n: kind of (= rather) 20
kit: first-aid kit 48
knife 52
knit v 40
knock down 23
known past part 100

L
lab technician 38
lamp 16
lantern 48
lasagna 46
lately 82
laugh v *61
laundry 94
    do the laundry 94
law *44
lbs. (= pounds) *13
leak v 106
lease n 106
leather 15
left s past 97
lemon 52
lemonade 51
lend 20
lens: contact lenses 87
less *88
lesson 43
letter: cover letter *98
lettuce 47
license: driver's license 56
life 100
light (= not serious) 103
lighter fluid 47
like (prep)
    like what? 48
    look like 13
line (of people) *81
linen (household articles) 16
list n *47C
local *78
lock n 106
long adj 14
    for a long time 101
long n: before long *44
look intrans 17
    look like 13
    look out 23
    look through 21
lost s past 21
lottery 56
lovely 27

_____ Acknowledgements _____

We wish to thank the following for providing us with photographs:

Page 6, *left:* Brunswick Bowling and Billiards Corp., *right:* Milton Bradley Company, a wholly owned subsidiary of Hasbro, Inc. **Page 8,** Courtesy of State Taxi, Photo by Heinz Paul Piper. **Page 17:** Photos by Heinz Paul Piper. **Page 26,** N.Y. Daily News photo. **Page 33,** N.Y. Convention and Visitors Bureau. **Page 41,** *Pic 1:* Pittsburgh Pirates; *Pic 2:* Photo by Evelyn Hofer; *Pic 3:* Photo # 306-NT-33204-V from The National Archives. **Page 44,** Photo #306-NT-33204-V from the National Archives. **Page 52,** Photos by Heinz Paul Piper. **Page 61,** Joyce Dopkeen, NYT Pictures. **Page 63,** Toronto Convention and Visitors Bureau. **Page 66,** Courtesy of Sears Roebuck & Co. **Page 76,** *Pic 1:* Lichtenstein, Roy, *Drowning Girl,* 1963. Oil and synthetic polymer paint on canvas, $67\frac{5}{8} \times 66\frac{3}{4}''$ (171.6×169.5 cm). Collection, The Museum of Modern Art, New York. Philip Johnson Fund (by exchange) and gift of Mr. and Mrs. Bagley Wright; *Pic 2:* Pollock, Jackson, *Number 1, 1948,* 1948. Oil on canvas, $68'' \times 8'8''$ (172.7×264.2 cm). Collection, The Museum of Modern Art, New York. Purchase; *Pic 3:* © The Prado Museum, Madrid, all rights reserved, total or partial reproduction prohibited. © S.P.A.D.E.M., Paris/ V.A.G.A., New York, 1986; *Pic 4:* © 1983, The Metropolitan Museum of Art, Rogers Fund, 1952; *Pic 5:* © 1982, The Metropolitan Museum of Art, gift of The Dillon Fund, 1973. **Page 78,** Photo by Nancy Perry. **Page 79,** Photo by Nancy Perry. **Page 84,** *Pic 1:* N.Y. Convention and Visitors Bureau; *Pic 2:* Marmot Mountain Works; *Pic 3:* Courtesy Harley-Davidson, Inc.; *Pic 4:* NASA; *Pic 5:* N.Y. Convention and Visitors Bureau; *Pic 6:* Photo by Heinz Paul Piper. **Page 87,** *left to right:* Pics 1 and 2: Courtesy of Sterling Optical; *Pic 3:* Courtesy of Ektelon. **Page 97,** Photo by Heinz Paul Piper.